Policy Transfer and
British Social Policy

Public Policy and Management

Series Editor: Professor R.A.W. Rhodes, Department of Politics, University of Newcastle.

The effectiveness of public policies is a matter of public concern and the efficiency with which policies are put into practice is a continuing problem for governments of all political persuasions. This series contributes to these debates by publishing informed, in-depth and contemporary analyses of public administration, public policy and public management.

The intention is to go beyond the usual textbook approach to the analysis of public policy and management and to encourage authors to move debate about their issue forward. In this sense, each book describes current thinking and research and explores future policy directions. Accessibility is a key feature and, as a result, the series will appeal to academics and their students as well as to the informed practitioner.

Current titles include:

Policy Transfer and British Social Policy

Learning from the USA?

David P. Dolowitz
with Rob Hulme, Mike Nellis and Fiona O'Neill

Open University Press
Buckingham · Philadelphia

Open University Press
Celtic Court
22 Ballmoor
Buckingham
MK18 1XW

e-mail: enquiries@openup.co.uk
world wide web: http://www.openup.co.uk

and

325 Chestnut Street
Philadelphia, PA 19106, USA

First Published 2000

A catalogue record of this book is available from the British Library

ISBN   0 335 19992 5 (hb)   0 335 19991 7 (pb)

Library of Congress Cataloging-in-Publication Data
Dolowitz, David P.
    Policy transfer and British social policy : learning from the
USA? / David P. Dolowitz with Rob Hulme, Mike Nellis, and Fiona
O'Neill.
        p.   cm.   (Public policy and management)
    Includes bibliographical references and index.
    ISBN 0-335-19992-5 (hb)
    ISBN 0-335-19991-7 (pb)
    1. Great Britain – Social policy 1979.   2. United States – Social
policy.   3. Public welfare – Great Britain.   4. Public welfare – United
States.   5. Welfare state.   6. Policy sciences.   I. Title.   II. Series.
    HN385.5. D65   1999
    361.6'1'0941–dc21   99–29252
                                                                              CIP

Typeset by Graphicraft Limited, Hong Kong
Printed in Great Britain by Biddles Ltd, Guildford and King's Lynn

To my family and friends
Thanks for the support!

Contents

Acknowledgements

I would like to thank Paul Rickerson, Dean Workman, Sharon Kiuhara and Sandra Snow for providing support and friendship and having faith in the face of adversity. I would like to send a special thanks to Robert J. Dean for sparking my interest in learning and showing me that the study of politics could actually be interesting. Dave Marsh – what else can I say? Thank you for the hours of work and mentoring. A well-deserved thanks must also go to Rachel King for helping maintain my sanity during the production of this work and for her editorial help. As usual, I would also like to thank my friends and family for their support over the past few years while this project has come to maturity. Finally, a warm and well-deserved thanks must go to Rod Rhodes and the staff at Open University Press for their excellent production and editorial work.

List of abbreviations

ACOP	Association of Chief Officers of Probation
ADC	Aid to Dependent Children
AFDC	Aid to Families with Dependent Children
ASI	Adam Smith Institute
BMA	British Medical Association
BMJ	*British Medical Journal*
BTEC	Business and Technical Education Council
CPS	Centre for Policy Studies
CSA	Child Support Agency
CSAS	Child Support Assurance System
CSEA	Child Support Enforcement Agency (America)
CSES	Child Support Enforcement System (America)
CVCP	Committee of Vice-Chancellors and Principals
DES	Department of Education and Science
DfEE	Department for Education and Employment
DoH	Department of Health
DSS	Department of Social Security
DHA	District Health Authority
EITC	Earned Income Tax Credit (America)
ERA	Education Reform Act (1988)
ET	Employment Training Scheme
EU	European Union
FEFCE	Further Education Funding Council for England
FSA	Family Support Act (1988)

FTES	Full time equivalent student
GP	General Practitioner
HEFCE	Higher Education Funding Council for England
HMI	Her Majesty's Inspectorate
HMO	Health Maintenance Organization
HMP	Her Majesty's Prison
IEA	Institute of Economic Affairs
IFI	International Financial Institutions
IGO	International Governing Organization
IMF	International Monetary Fund
IPPR	Institute for Public Policy Research
IT	Information Technology
JSA	Job Seeker's Allowance
NACRO	National Association for the Care and Rehabilitation of Offenders
NAPO	National Association of Probation Officers
NGO	Non-Governmental Organization
NHS	National Health Service
NVQ	National Vocational Qualification
OBRA	Omnibus Budget Reconciliation Act (America)
OECD	Organization for Economic Co-operation and Development
Ofsted	Office for Standards in Education
OTA	Offender Tag Association
PPi	Progressive Policy Institute
PRWOA	Personal Responsibility and Work Opportunity Act (America)
PSBR	Public Sector Borrowing Requirement
QA	Quality Audit
RAE	Research Assessment Exercise
TANF	Temporary Assistance to Needy Families (America)
TEC	Training and Enterprise Council
TEFRA	Tax Equity and Fiscal Responsibility Act (America)
TNC	Transnational Corporation
TTA	Teacher Training Agency
W-2	Wisconsin Works (America)
WFTC	Working Families Tax Credit (UK)
WFP	*Working for Patients* (White Paper)
WHO	World Health Organization
WIN	Work Incentive Program (America)

Introduction: a new face to British public policy

Over the past twenty years the British state has undergone fundamental transformations in most areas of public policy, particularly those associated with social policy: welfare, health, education, and law and order. The purpose of this book is to develop and then use a model of policy transfer to illustrate how many of the changes in British public policy during the 1980s and 1990s can be traced directly to the process of policy transfer, particularly policy transfer between the United States and Britain. At the outset it should be understood that, while there are difficulties in any attempt to carry out and analyse international policy transfer, this book demonstrates that in numerous areas of social policy, policy makers in Britain and the United States were able to overcome these difficulties. At the same time, each contributor to this volume also demonstrates that, while policy makers were able to engage in policy transfer from the US to Britain, problems emerged due to the process of transfer itself. Particularly influential in the emergence of problems was policy makers' failure to adapt American (and other foreign) models appropriately to their new setting, despite continual claims that they understood the importance of adapting 'foreign' models before implementing them.[1]

Why use policy transfer to analyse public policy?

It is necessary to analyse the development of British public policy, especially its social policy component, through the eyes of policy transfer because, while there have been many studies examining British public and social policy, there has not been nearly enough work done in this field. Of the work that has been carried out in this field almost none has examined it through a policy transfer perspective. Moreover, when scholars have conducted comparative public and social policy studies, particularly between the United States and Britain, they have tended to overlook the possibility that American policies could act as models for other political systems. Worse, they have tended to make broad generalizations, which careful research has shown to be false.

For example, because many scholars of the welfare state assume, and even argue, that there is something unique about American social policy, few have attempted to examine, or even seen the validity of examining, how the American welfare state has influenced other political systems (for good examples see Marmor *et al.* 1990; Skocpol 1992, 1995). Because of this, it is commonly argued that the American welfare system lags far behind the welfare systems found in other welfare states, including Britain. However, using a model of policy transfer to analyse the development of British public policy, this book will demonstrate that this generalization is false. Ginsburg has provided a much more accurate description of the situation:

> Up to the 1980s, supporters of the West European welfare state . . . saw the US welfare state developing to catch up with Western Europe. It is very important to discard such notions . . . The fact is that the US welfare state since the 1930s has been a viable, working model . . . which ranks alongside the European models in status and significance.
>
> (Ginsburg 1992: 98)

By developing and applying a model of policy transfer this book will demonstrate that America has viable and working models of social policy at the federal and state levels. More importantly, this volume will demonstrate that these models have been a source of ideas, inspirations, policies and institutions for various aspects of British public policy over the past twenty years (for a detailed examination of the American influence on the development of British welfare-to-work policies during the Thatcher era see Dolowitz 1998).

Given the above, and the fact that the transfer of ideas, policies and institutions between the United States and Britain has been attracting attention since Prime Minister Thatcher's first government, one of the most crucial tasks this book sets out to perform is to explain why British policy makers turned to the United States instead of other viable alternatives. In other words, if the US is 'unique', why would British policy makers turn to America instead of a more similar system? By applying the policy transfer framework established in Chapter 1, the contributors to this volume will help explain why Britain turned to the United States and to a lesser extent Australia and New Zealand instead of Europe for policies, programmes, ideas and inspirations.[2]

What is policy transfer?

Given the importance of policy transfer in the development of British public policy over the past twenty years one must ask what the policy transfer process consists of. While this question is addressed in Chapter 1, for the moment let it be noted that, for the past decade, there has been a growing body of literature which uses, discusses and analyses the processes involved in lesson drawing, policy convergence, policy diffusion and policy transfer. While the terminology and focus of each of these bodies of literature varies, in one way or another all of these studies are concerned with a similar process. As such, it seems that a relatively uncontentious definition of the process, and more specifically, policy transfer, is: the occurrence of, and processes involved in, the development of programmes, policies, institutions, etc. within one political and/or social system which are based upon the ideas, institutions, programmes and policies emanating from other political and/or social systems.

However, it must be stressed that, while there has been a growing interest in policy transfer over the past two decades, it has always existed. For example, Handa (1959) clearly illustrated the role voluntary and coercive transfer played in the spread of ideas, policies and programmes across Europe and the Middle East during the Hellenistic period. Similarly, Waltman (1980) demonstrated the importance policy transfer played in the development of the American income tax system during the Civil War. Heclo (1974) has shown the role and impact of policy transfer on the development of social policies in Britain and Sweden, while more recently, Dolowitz (1998) demonstrated how the development of the British workfare state depended upon programmes, policies and institutions existing within the United States, Canada and Sweden during the 1980s and 1990s.

Just as policy transfer has always existed, the rapid growth in communications of all types, combined with the dramatic increase in the number of international organizations since the middle of the twentieth century, has accelerated the process. Such changes have both increased the amount of information available to policy makers and made it almost a requirement that they know what is going on elsewhere. So, for example, in response to the widely publicized 'fact' that the Clinton administration has been 'successful' at reducing levels of unemployment in America, many European governments have contacted Robert Reich, President Clinton's former head of employment policy, for advice.

The rapid growth in global communications is not the only pressure towards policy transfer; global economic forces are also having a dramatic impact. As the globalization literature demonstrates, it is difficult, if not impossible, for any nation in the industrialized or industrializing world to protect its political, social or even economic structures from trends going on elsewhere. Thus, as international integration becomes institutionalized, policy makers will increasingly have to look to other political systems for ideas, programmes and policies; cues as to what will or will not work; and ideas about what is, and is not, internationally acceptable. Parsons captures the essence of this (1995: 234):

> As the world economy in particular is transformed by new modes of production and trade, and as transnational corporations and institutions

come to exercise more influence and power, so the capacity of national policy-makers to frame their own agendas is diminished. Public policy now takes place in a world system as well as in national political systems.

Together these changes, by subjecting countries to similar pressures and expanding the amount of information available to policy makers, have meant that they are increasingly looking to other political systems for knowledge and ideas on how to change their own political system.

Not surprisingly, the increase in both the occurrence of, and interest in, policy transfer has led proponents of comparative politics, public policy, social policy and developmental studies to begin using the concept within their own work. For example, Cox (1993) has analysed the role played by lesson drawing within the development of Czechoslovakia's and Hungary's post-communist welfare systems. More recently, Campbell (1993, 1996) demonstrated that when the International Monetary Fund (IMF) attempted to impose neo-liberal economic and social policies on Poland, Hungary and Czechoslovakia, the institutional legacies left over from their communist past led to substantially different policy outcomes. Similarly, work is beginning to establish the links between European health care reforms and the lessons they have taught, and can teach, Latin and South American countries (Salazar 1997).[3]

Not only is international policy transfer occurring on a regular basis but, as the case studies within this volume demonstrate, it is having real impacts on the development of programmes, policies and even entire political systems in a variety of countries. Countries ranging from Azerbaijan to Zambia are turning to other countries in the development of national policies, programmes and institutions. When engaging in policy transfer, governments need not look to the most obvious of places. For example, one of the models the Blair government is looking to in its attempt to reform the British pension system is Chile. Similarly, it has been clearly documented that while developing its proposals to get single parents back to work the Blair government looked to countries as diverse, both politically and geographically, as Australia (the JET Programme) and America (Personal Responsibility and Work Opportunity Act of 1996) for inspiration and ideas. They even turned to Wisconsin Works (W-2), the hardcore workfare programme developed and implemented under the conservative administration of Governor Tommy Thompson, for ideas and inspirations.

Given that policy transfer is occurring globally, on a regular basis, and that it is having real world impacts, it is necessary to develop a model capable of generating a series of questions which can be generalized across academic disciplines and issue areas. Once such a model has been established it should be possible to examine the theoretical and empirical validity of the model. This will allow academics to develop a workable theory of why, when and how governments use policy transfer and what consequences this may have for the outcomes of policy decisions (early attempts at developing typologies of policy transfer can be seen in Bennett 1991, 1992; Rose 1993; Dolowitz and Marsh 1996).

What is this book claiming about policy transfer?

Let me be clear about what this book is claiming. First, it suggests that an increasing amount of policy development, and particularly policy change, in contemporary polities like Britain is affected by policy transfer. As such, when analysing public policies we always need to ask the question, Is policy transfer involved? If so, a second question which needs to be addressed is, What has its impact been on the policy in question?

Second, some countries seem more subject to policy transfer than others; in particular, the United States seems to feature much more as a lender than as a borrower, and this is one of the key reasons it features heavily within the case studies presented within this volume. At the same time, as this book will illustrate, in most areas of public policy Britain appears to be a borrower, although this is not a hard and fast rule. For example, as Hulme's chapter demonstrates, in at least the area of education Britain has been one of the key global policy exporters. Similarly, Nellis demonstrates that contrary to the accepted wisdom a modified version of the English day centres for adult offenders was transferred to America from Britain during the 1980s, even though, as this volume will demonstrate, this was perceived as the quintessential period for American exports to the UK (McDevitt and Miliano 1992). Thus, it cannot be assumed that transfer is omnipresent. This said, it is clear from the cases presented within this volume that at least in the field of social policy some countries are more likely to borrow while some countries are more likely to lend. As such, it needs to be established why some countries, such as the United States, are frequent 'lenders' while others, such as Britain, are frequently 'borrowers'.

One variable which helps explain why the United States was capable of exporting social policy models to Britain over the past twenty years was the rise of the New Right in both countries during the 1970s. Or as Savage, Atkinson and Robins (1994: xi) argue, 'if anything the influence of New Right thought and ideology has been more in evidence since the departure of Margaret Thatcher as Prime Minister than before, this despite the relatively low key nature of political rhetoric which has characterized post-Thatcher Conservative leadership'. While the rise of the New Right is important in itself, it cannot explain the UK's dependence on American models; for this, other variables must be found. One of these is the liberal nature of both the American and British welfare regimes. This similarity has always made the US and the UK natural bedfellows when it comes to ideas and policies surrounding the welfare state and human nature (see Epsing-Andersen 1990, 1996).[4] While the structural similarity, revolving around the liberal regime and the rise of the New Right in the United States and Britain, can help account for some of the reasons why the Thatcher, Major and even Blair governments have turned to the United States, they do not account for everything. Thus, a further variable which emerges from the pages of this volume is the importance of the 'special relationship', or perceived affinities, between Washington and London. There can be little dispute that the close personal relationship which existed between Thatcher and

Reagan, and exists between Clinton and Blair, has encouraged British policy makers to borrow American ideas and policies.

Third, this book will demonstrate that policy transfer is an important area to study because it is a critical variable in the failure, or perceived failure, of an increasing number of national and international policies, programmes and institutions. An important component of this 'failure', not previously mentioned, is the fact that when policies and programmes are borrowed, policy makers tend to adapt them to their own social, cultural and institutional setting. While this might seem like the rational choice, this process of adaptation often leads to a different pattern of implementation and policy development, and thus to a set of problems not encountered in the originating country. However, as previously mentioned, this is not the sole cause of problems found within this volume. For example, the case study on the British Child Support Agency demonstrates the corollary to this. More precisely, because the Thatcher and Major governments decided not to adapt the American system, and more specifically the Wisconsin Child Support model, to the existing British cultural and institutional settings it led to actual administrative and operational problems and perceived operational failure among politicians, clients and the public.

Fourth, as will be discussed in Chapter 1, this book is not arguing that policy transfer can be used entirely as an independent variable, explaining why policy makers turned to transfer or how a policy was actually implemented into a new setting. Rather, it must be used as both an independent and a dependent variable. Occasionally it can be argued that a policy or programme in one setting was so widely perceived as being the 'best' that policy makers adopted it into their own system. Normally a combination of factors, often completely separate from the actual policies, programme or institution in question, drives policy makers to turn to policy transfer. Moreover, while policy transfer might be of use in explaining where an idea came from, under most circumstances it cannot be used to explain how borrowed policy or programmes are changed and adapted once placed into a new setting. Thus, as will be returned to in the conclusion, truly to understand the power of the policy transfer concept it needs to be combined with other macro-level and micro-level theories of policy development.

A new approach to British public policy

To understand the process of policy transfer and its importance to the development of British public policy during the 1980s and 1990s this book will examine four case studies: the development of the British Child Support Agency (CSA); transformations within the National Health Service (NHS); changes to the British post-compulsory education system; and the development of the British electronic tagging policy. However, before any discussion of policy transfer and the development of public policy can be undertaken one must first understand what policy transfer consists of and subsequently identify some of the key mechanisms involved in the transfer process. Thus, Chapter 1 will develop a model of policy transfer (adapted from Dolowitz and Marsh 1996; Dolowitz 1998) capable of generating a series of questions which can then be used in the analysis of British public policy. It will identify the key actors and elements involved in the process. More importantly, it will discuss some of the major factors which help facilitate (or restrict) the policy transfer process. Chapter 1 also explores some of the primary techniques and resources researchers can use to establish that policy transfer was involved in the development of a policy, programme, institution or idea. The chapter also includes a brief discussion on how the policy transfer process can be coupled with the literature on policy making to enhance our overall understanding of the policy-making process.

Chapter 2 begins the detailed case study portion of this volume with an examination of the British Child Support Agency. Here it is argued that the Thatcher government borrowed both the institutional structure and major functions of the British CSA from the United States. As part of this, Chapter 2 also illustrates that the Thatcher government justified its decision to borrow the Agency from the US based upon its understanding of how the Australian CSA was itself borrowed from America. Importantly, the chapter also discusses the factors which drove the Thatcher government to look to the United States in the development of the CSA and how the actual process of policy transfer can help explain why the Agency was almost universally perceived as a 'failure'. The chapter concludes with a brief examination of some of the subsequent changes the Major and Blair governments introduced, or have proposed, drawing attention to the fact that many of these proposals have themselves emerged out of the process of policy transfer.

Chapter 3 examines two of the major changes which occurred in the National Health Service during the 1980s and 1990s: the development of the 'internal market' and the gradual implementation of the 'managed care' system. Unlike Chapter 2, this chapter demonstrates that while the Thatcher–Major governments drew lessons from the US health system, policy transfer cannot be used as a independent variable to explain why the United States was used as the model for British health reforms. Rather, Chapter 3 demonstrates that while American ideas influenced the content of British reforms, the ideas were not themselves 'inherently attractive'. Rather, it was the desire to reduce the overall public sector borrowing requirement, and particularly health care budgets, in combination with the need to respond to the developments in medical technology that drove the Conservative governments to engage in policy transfer.

Chapter 4 explores the role of policy transfer in the development of British post-compulsory education policy. This chapter demonstrates that major changes in the ideological, economic and political structure of the British state led policy makers to turn to both the 'past' and the American higher education system for lessons. Chapter 4 also argues that, while institutional and structural reforms were transferred, these ideas were 'filtered' and reshaped to fit the existing domestic situation. Moreover, the chapter demonstrates that many of the reforms instituted as a result of policy transfer had unintended consequences which forced policy makers to continue adapting the system in ways that have brought it ever closer to the American system of higher education.

Chapter 5 concludes the case study segment of this volume with an examination of the 'Americanization' of British penal policy. Specifically, Chapter 5 examines the development of the English electronic monitoring programme (no similar systems have been established in Wales or Scotland prior to the publication of this book). This chapter demonstrates that, while electronic monitoring was an American import, once it arrived, American rhetoric and programmes were repackaged and sold as 'British'. Importantly, this chapter also examines the role of the Prison Service in initially acting as a block on the transfer and implementation of the American 'tagging' programme.

Chapter 6 draws together all the major themes found within this volume. In particular, Chapter 6 argues that, while policy transfer is indeed an important aspect to consider when looking at the development and 'failure' of British public policy over the past twenty years, if it is combined with other meso-level, micro-level and even macro-level theories its explanatory power is greatly increased. Moreover, Chapter 6 demonstrates that when policy transfer is linked to traditional theories of public policy and the policy-making process their explanatory power can be significantly enhanced.

1

Policy transfer: a new framework of policy analysis

David P. Dolowitz

Clearly all governments are using 'foreign' models in the development of national programmes, policies, institutions, structures, etc. It is also clear that the occurrence of policy transfer is increasing, and will continue to increase, as market, communication and technological advances make it cheaper and easier to obtain information about other systems. As this has happened, a growing body of literature has emerged which stresses the process by which knowledge of ideas, institutions, policies and programmes in one setting is fed into the policy-making arena in the development and change of policies and programmes in another setting. However, while some studies have developed which describe this process and others which use it to explain the development of a policy, programme, institution or even an entire political system, there have been few attempts to organize the elements of this phenomenon into a coherent model capable of being generalized across policy areas and academic disciplines. The aim of this chapter is to present such a model which will then be used throughout the book to illustrate various instances of policy transfer in the transformation of the modern British state.

The model presented in this chapter builds upon the work of Dolowitz and Marsh (1996) and Dolowitz (1998) by asking a series of nine questions illustrated in Table 1.1: Why and when do actors engage in policy transfer? Who transfers policy? What is transferred? From where are lessons drawn? Are there different degrees of transfer? When do actors engage in policy transfer and how does this affect the policy-making and policy transfer processes? What restricts policy transfer? How can researchers begin demonstrating the occurrence of policy transfer? How can policy transfer help our understanding of policy failure?

Table 1.1 A policy transfer framework

Why transfer? Continuum Want to → Have to Voluntary · Mixtures · Coercive	Who is involved in transfer?	What is transferred?	From where?			Degrees of transfer	Constraints on transfer	How to demonstrate policy transfer	How transfer leads to policy failure
			Past	Within-a-nation	Cross-national				
Lesson drawing (Perfect rationality)	Elected officials	Policies (goals) (content) (instruments)	Internal	State governments	International organizations	Copying	Policy complexity	Media (newspaper) (magazine) (TV) (radio) (internet)	Uninformed transfer
Lesson drawing (Bounded rationality)	Bureaucrats/ Civil servants	Programmes	Global	City governments	National/ Local governments	Emulation	Past policies	Reports (commissioned) (uncommissioned)	Incomplete transfer
International pressures (image) (consensus) (perceptions)	Pressure groups	Institutions		Local governments		Mixtures	Structural/ Institutional	Conferences	Inappropriate transfer
Conditionality (Loans) (Conditions attached to business activity)	Political parties	Ideologies			Local governments	Inspiration	Feasibility (ideology) (cultural proximity) (technology) (economic) (bureaucratic)	Meetings/Visits	
Obligations	Policy entrepreneurs/ Experts	Attitudes/ Cultural values					Language	Statements (written) (verbal)	
Direct imposition	Consultants/ Think tanks	Negative lessons					Past relations		
	Transnational corporations								
	Supranational institutions								

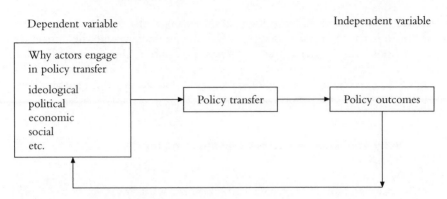

Figure 1.1 Policy transfer uncoupled
Source: adapted from Dolowitz 1998: 176.

It could be argued that generating a series of questions is of limited utility; that, at best, it provides a way of organizing research but does not show that the concept has explanatory power. However, as the chapters in this volume demonstrate, there are clearly problems with such an argument. Of course, policy transfer can be treated as either a dependent or an independent variable; it can seek to explain the process of policy transfer or it can be used to explain policy outcomes. However, as illustrated in Figure 1.1, the two exercises are related. Put simply, if one wishes to use policy transfer to explain policy outcomes, then one also needs to explain what causes transfer. Thus, a full analysis treats policy transfer as both a dependent and an independent variable. This point is easily illustrated. Why a lesson is drawn, where a lesson is drawn from and who is involved in the transferring process all affect whether transfer occurs and whether that transfer is successful. So, for example, if a government searches hurriedly for a solution to an urgent 'problem', it may be more likely that there will be a transfer, because the need for a 'solution' is imperative, but less likely that the transfer will be successful, because limited time will inevitably lead to a limited search for models, inappropriate alterations, or even no adaptations. Thus, this situation will probably lead to a situation where the entire process is fraught with problems. Similarly, if the search for a policy involves not only politicians and bureaucrats, but also the key interest groups representing those affected by the transfer, while the transfer process may be more complicated, there may well be fewer implementation problems once the policy is transferred. The key point is that in order to use policy transfer as an explanatory variable, one also needs to understand and explain the process of transfer; focusing on the questions which form the basis of the policy transfer framework presented in this chapter and illustrated in Table 1.1 allows us to begin understanding these processes.

Overall, this chapter has two key aims: first, it develops the model of analysis used throughout the remainder of this book. It provides the setting used to explain how policy transfer influenced the changes observed in various areas of British social and public policy. Second, in conjunction with the remainder of the book, this chapter will demonstrate the utility of the concept of policy transfer, in particular its usefulness in helping to provide a greater understanding of the content and development of various aspects of British social policy during the 1980s and 1990s.

Why and when do actors engage in policy transfer?

When studying policy transfer we need to know what drives actors to engage in the process. This information helps explain why different policy makers look to particular models and nations rather than others. More importantly, knowing why actors turn to policy transfer can help explain why it often appears that governments implement policies and programmes inappropriate to a given situation. Given this, it is crucial to begin this section by briefly distinguishing between voluntary and coercive transfer, treating them as two ideal-type end points on a continuum (see Figure 1.2). Purely voluntary transfer occurs when political actors make a 'rational' and 'conscious' decision to borrow policies, programmes, etc. from another time and/or political system. In contrast, purely coercive transfer occurs when one or more political systems or international organizations impose a policy, programme or institutional reform upon another political system. Of course between these two extremes there are other categories characterized by more or less voluntary and coercive elements. Finally, how a lesson is used often depends upon the audience addressed. For example, while the Thatcher, Major and Blair governments admitted on many occasions that they were drawing lessons, in the development of the British welfare-to-work system, from both the past and the United States during Parliamentary debates and in personal interviews, they rarely admitted this influence in public statements or press releases (Dolowitz 1998).

Furthermore, it should be stressed at the outset that this continuum is a heuristic device. I am not arguing that the categories are equidistant from one another or that any case of transfer will fit precisely into any category. Rather, the continuum has been designed to allow the researchers within this volume, and anyone interested in this field more generally, to think systematically about the types of, and processes involved in, policy transfer. This continuum helps for two related reasons. First, it identifies categories which can be used by researchers to frame their empirical work. Second, many cases of transfer involve both voluntary and coercive elements; the continuum helps us acknowledge that fact, and thus deepens our knowledge of the process. For example, knowing that a case of policy transfer involved coercive and voluntary elements, as was the case with Britain's adoption of American-style workfare during the 1980s and 1990s, it should be possible to see how its pattern of diffusion changed from this point. For instance, it is clear that since Britain's initial adoption of

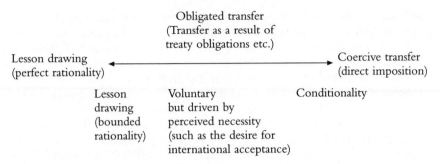

Figure 1.2 From lesson drawing to coercive transfer

American style workfare, European countries have begun looking at American and British workfare programmes. Some, such as Belgium, were doing so voluntarily; others, such as Norway, were doing so because of the perception among key policy makers that they were falling behind an international trend. As this example demonstrates, by using a continuum, researchers can capture some of the subtleties involved in the transfer process, such as if the transfer remained voluntary or transformed into a more coercive process over time, or even varied between different political units within the same political system or across systems.

To begin, at the purely voluntary end of the continuum is lesson drawing. Lesson drawing is based upon the view that actors actively, and willingly, choose policy transfer as a rational response to a 'perceived problem' or undesirable condition. In this view, policy transfer occurs when policy makers perceive a condition as being problematic, or when 'dissatisfaction with the status quo' arises. When this happens policy makers will rationally and voluntarily engage in an active search for new ideas as a 'cheap' means of solving the problem. As Rose puts it: 'The process of lesson-drawing starts with scanning programmes in effect elsewhere, and ends with the prospective evaluation of what would happen if a programme already in effect elsewhere were transferred here in future' (Rose 1991: 3).

There are clear problems with this analysis for it is rare that any actors are perfectly rational. Most act with limited information, are influenced by their perceptions of a particular decision-making situation rather than the 'real' situation, and are constrained by the set of institutional and structural confines in which they find themselves. Moreover, there is no doubt that public problems are not just out there 'waiting to be dealt with'. Rather, when engaging in voluntary policy transfer it is necessary for policy makers to perceive an existing situation or condition as a problem, for policy making is not only about developing and implementing policies and programmes; it is about defining public problems in the first place. Or as Anderson (1978: 20) argues, 'Whether a nation perceives poverty, inflation or unemployment as a problem or merely a condition depends on the standards of judgement and the ideals employed by policy-makers when making political evaluations.' Thus, before policy transfer can occur, policy makers must first define a condition as a public problem, rather than a private issue or a complete non-issue. This itself depends upon the mix of issues and events occurring at any given time. This mix is important because it will shape which conditions policy makers will want to elevate to the problem level; which of these they are going to deal with at a public level; and how they are going to deal with them. As such, both the decision to engage in policy transfer and how policy makers engage in that transfer may be based upon an inaccurate or biased assessment of the 'real' situation.[5] Thus transfer is often driven within the confines of what Simon (1957) refers to as 'bounded rationality' or Lindblom (1979) refers to as 'incrementalism' or 'disjointed incrementalism'.

Another factor driving policy transfer lying closer to the centre of the policy transfer continuum is perceptual policy transfer. One of the more common causes of this is when actors within one policy-making system perceive their system as falling behind its primary competitors. In this scenario, while policy makers look to their primary competitors for lessons it is not a purely rational or voluntary process. Rather they are acting within psychological and practical constraints. Moreover, under this scenario, when looking for lessons the search is limited to what policy makers perceive as the best practice of their primary competitors, often with little understanding of how it works in the originating system or how it will work in its new setting.

Another perceptual cause lying nearer the centre of the continuum are cases in which actors turn to policy transfer because they believe that this action will make their system internationally 'recognized' or 'acceptable'. The reason actors can turn to policy transfer in this situation is because it is often the case that the international community 'agrees' on a best practice or solution to particular problem. Thus countries adopting this solution can improve their status within the international community. For example, John Campbell (1997: 5) found:

> some [post-communist countries] sought to harmonize their tax structures with those of their West Europe neighbors in an effort to appear westernized and legitimate thereby increasing their chances of being accepted into various international organizations and accords.

Nations may turn voluntarily to policy transfer, seeing it as the best solution. However, if a problem and its perceived solution have been internationally defined and agreed upon, a nation which does not adopt this solution will face increasing pressure to join the international community. So, as mentioned, Norway's decision to develop American/British style workfare programmes provides an excellent example of the way international pressure can force political actors to adopt policies perceived to be in place elsewhere, even when it appears there is little need for them based upon the existing political, cultural and/or economic situations in the borrowing system.[6]

Moving towards the coercive end of the continuum, actors in one setting can be 'pushed' to adopt foreign models as a result of the actions of external actors or events. There is clear evidence that externalities are leading policy makers to engage in policy transfer in many areas of policy, including environmental and labour market regulations. For example, in a speech to the Socialist Leaders' Congress in Malmo, Sweden, 6 June 1997, Britain's Prime Minister Tony Blair argued that Britain and Europe needed to retain flexible labour market policies within the European employment chapter so that they would not be at a disadvantage in relation to the economic challenges presented by the 'tiger economies' of South East Asia (Sherman 1997).

Nearer the purely coercive end of the continuum can be identified cases in which transnational corporations (TNCs) and international aid agencies are able to compel governments, even the governments of Western industrialized nations, to adopt programmes and policies against their will, as a condition of their continuous presence or aid. In these situations, because TNCs and aid agencies use specified conditions to force policy makers to turn to transfer, this type of policy transfer can be referred to as conditional.

Transnational corporations can force policy makers into policy transfer by attaching conditions to their decisions to locate within a particular country. For example, Fundanga and Mwaba (1997: 24) demonstrate that:

> Heinz's offer to take a stake in a Zambian parastatal in the food processing industry was rejected on the basis that the offer was low. Heinz quickly moved to a neighbouring country where a similar offer was accepted. Heinz not only buys the processed farm produce (and exports) in that country, but the company helps the suppliers with advanced farming practices to get the best yields [technology transfer].

International lending agencies have a similar power in that they can, and do, attach conditions to the loans they provide. For example, it has been well documented that international aid organizations have often 'forced' Western economic and social policies upon third world and post-communist governments as a condition of the granting of a loan (Hague *et al.* 1992; Campbell 1997).

Moving on, governments can also be forced into adopting programmes and policies as part of their obligations as members of international regimes and structures. For example, within the European Union (EU), member states are required to adapt their national policies to match European regulations and directives as part of their obligations to the Union. It is worth pointing out that there are problems with such a classification. For example, within the EU, the Court of Justice can 'force' member states to comply with European policy as part of their obligations to the Union. However, since individual nations voluntarily joined the Union, can any act of the EU be considered coercive in terms of policy transfer? Moreover, since each nation has influence over the adoption of EU policies, they actively and voluntarily shape any policy the Court may impose upon them. It is for these reasons that this type of transfer is best viewed as obligated, since it occurs as a result of obligations made prior to the occurrence of any actual policy transfer.

Finally, the most coercive case of policy transfer occurs when one government, political institution or political system forces another to adopt a programme, policy or institutional structure. For example, after World War II the American government drafted the Japanese constitution and was heavily involved in the development of various sections of the German constitution. As Majone (1991: 88) discussed: 'At the end of November 1952, the experts of the High Commission sent the German government a draft which was based on the German submission but contained a number of more radical clauses inspired by [the] US.'

A brief examination of the development of the British workfare system can be used to illustrate the use of the continuum and how to locate a case study in relation to it. In the mid–1980s the Thatcher government began facing mounting electoral pressures due to an exponential rise in the level of unemployment and Britain's falling international competitiveness. The government's initial response was to adjust the unemployment statistics. However, as it became apparent that this was not working they turned to policy transfer from the US and Canada, initially developing the Restart Programme and opening Job Clubs. At this stage, the impetus for turning to policy transfer was a mixture of more or less voluntary and coercive forces. Certainly the fear of losing the next general election and falling behind the international market for jobs and products put pressure on the government to find solutions. However, even at this stage, the government had considerable autonomy as to whether it would respond to these emerging 'problems' and indeed where it would look for lessons. Over the next fourteen years the Thatcher, Major and Blair governments continued to borrow and implement various American-style workfare policies and programmes including the Employment Training Scheme (ET); Training and Enterprise Councils (TECs); the Job Seeker's Allowance (JSA); and most recently various elements of the New Deals for young and long-term unemployed individuals, communities and lone parents. Over this period, as unemployment statistics fell and the world economy transformed, the motivation underpinning the borrowing of American policies and programmes and, equally important, the decision about which policies to borrow and where to look has altered. The coercive pressures decreased and voluntary factors became more important. This can most clearly be seen in the Blair government's decision to implement the America Earned Income Tax Credit (EITC) as the Working Families' Tax Credit (WFTC) (which falls as close to the purely rational end of the continuum as a policy is ever likely to do) and examine the Scandinavian welfare states for ideas and possible policies.

Who transfers policy?

Although anyone within the policy-making process can theoretically participate in policy transfer, actors can basically be classified into nine main categories:

elected officials; bureaucrats and civil servants; policy entrepreneurs and experts; consultants; political parties; pressure groups; think tanks; corporations; and both governmental and non-governmental international organizations and institutions.

As will be clearly demonstrated throughout this volume, in most, but not all, policy areas, the principal group involved in policy transfer are elected officials, because: 'their values give direction to public policy and their endorsement is needed to legitimate the adoption of programs' (Rose 1993: 52). Moreover, as will be demonstrated, elected officials set the boundaries of acceptable policy during their administrations. In fact, it is probably impossible to implant an idea or policy, regardless of how much merit it may have or how many other countries are pursuing it, if key members of a government are opposed to it (see Bunce 1981). Even when other non-elected policy makers within a government want to pursue policy transfer, if politicians are too insular or ignorant of the possibilities presented by the process it is unlikely that anything will emerge – even if information was exchanged between non-elected officials and policy makers in another political system.

Closely associated with politicians are professionals, administrators and civil servants. In fact, in the process of policy transfer it is arguable that these groups are as important as politicians in the policy development stage and, possibly, more important during the implementation stages. Their importance goes beyond their role in the development of the details of policies and the implementation of programmes; administrators and civil servants are often crucial in the process of conveying the detailed information to policy makers in their own and other political systems. Thus not only must the correct administrators and civil servants be found (which may not be as easy as it sounds) but they must be *willing* and *able* to discuss the details of policies and programmes with domestic and foreign policy makers. Often, government regulations will prevent these actors from communicating information to interested policy makers. Moreover, even when administrators and civil servants are allowed to speak to 'foreign' policy makers they often convey a 'sanitized' version of reality. It is probable that this has brought about, and will continue to bring about, many of the implementation problems experienced by political systems engaging in policy transfer. If foreign officials are not informed of the problems a particular policy or programme has encountered during its implementation process, and they borrow it in ignorance of these, they are likely to experience problems, if not similar problems, themselves.

Policy entrepreneurs are increasingly being discussed as key actors in the policy-making process. Specifically, entrepreneurs are people with an interest in a particular substantive area of policy and who are willing to 'invest their resources, time, energy, reputation, and sometimes money, in the hope of a future return' (Kingdon 1984: 129). Not only are policy entrepreneurs important in the process of policy making but they are clearly key players in the spread of ideas and policies between political systems. In fact, entrepreneurs are so important to the process of policy transfer that each of the case studies presented within this book explicitly points to the role of at least one entrepreneur in the development of the policy or institution in question. One interesting phenomenon is the role of the academic entrepreneur. Not only are academics advising local and national governments, but they are heavily involved in the work of international organizations and think tanks, often moving between these institutions throughout their careers. In each of these areas academic entrepreneurs take with them policy proposals, which are often accepted as legitimate due to their status as academics.

Policy makers at the local, national and international level of governance are increasingly relying on the advice of consultants, whether individuals or firms, who act as policy experts in the development of new programmes, policies and institutional structures. The role of policy consultants is particularly important because they tend to offer advice based on what they regard as the 'best' model or practice, often paying too little attention to the particular context in the originating or borrowing country. For example, Policy Management Groups are being set up in numerous African countries, with limited consideration of their appropriateness to the nation or given situation. They are being recommended for transfer into these countries simply because one particular consultancy firm has been pushing this model as a way for these countries to modernize their governing structures (Garnett 1997).

Of course, political consultants are not simply involved in the harmonization of political systems around the globe; their role in the policy transfer process is far more complex. For example, different national and international organizations can hire different consultants in their efforts to exert pressure on national governments. Not only does this pit different agencies and consultants against one another, but it means that national governments have room to decide which path to pursue, since they can pick and choose among the consultants' suggestions. As Bevan et al. argue:

> Most consultants to developing and transitional governments are contacted by donors; their consultancies are usually part of a larger donor programme over which they have no control. The lead . . . is usually taken by the international financial institutions (IFIs), particularly the World Bank, who currently exert considerable leverage through the conditionalities attached to their Structural Adjustment Loans. However, other international organizations (eg UNDP, the EU, the African Development Bank) and bilateral donors (eg ODA/DfID, NORAD, SIDA, etc) can take different lines, or try to modify the IFI approach, and they may do this through consultancies.
>
> (Bevan et al. 1997: 3–4)

Only individual agents of policy transfer have been discussed so far, but groups and organizations are also involved in the process. Obviously, political parties are constantly engaging in policy transfer because they need new ideas and policies to increase their electoral appeal and to appease party activists. Thus, in Chapter 5 Nellis discusses how the development of electronic monitoring got caught up in electoral politics, while Chapter 4 contrasts the role of policy transfer in the policies of the Conservative and Labour Parties towards post-secondary education. It must be noted that, as with individual politicians, parties tend to use lessons selectively, either to defend or to forward ideas and policies which advance their ideological beliefs and electoral chances, not necessarily to advance policies they intend to implement once in office.

Nationally and internationally based pressure (interest) groups are also involved in policy transfer as their sole purpose is to influence the policy-making process. Moreover, many groups keep in contact with groups in other political systems, exchanging ideas and drawing lessons from each other's experience. This information is then fed into the policy-making process through governmental contacts and public pressure. Probably the best example of the role pressure groups have played in policy transfer comes from Chapter 5, when Nellis discusses the role played by the National Association of Probation Officers (NAPO), the Association of Chief Officers of Probation (ACOP) and the Offender Tag Association (OTA) in the development of the UK's electronic monitoring programme.

As will be more fully illustrated in Chapters 3–5, during the 1980s and early 1990s think tanks, particularly neo-liberal think tanks (and more recently left-wing think tanks) began to spread their influence, both directly and indirectly, in the development of programmes and policies across the globe. Especially important in the transatlantic exchange of ideas during the Conservative administrations of Thatcher and Major were the US-based Heritage Foundation, the Cato Institute and the American Enterprise Institute (AEI). Interestingly for the process of policy transfer, these think tanks had both formal and informal links with the UK-based Institute of Economic Affairs (IEA), the Centre for Policy Studies (CPS) and the Adam Smith Institute (ASI). More recently the Blair government has been turning to liberal UK-based think tanks such as DEMOS and the Institute for Public Policy Research (IPPR), both of which have close links to American-based left-wing think tanks such as the Progressive Policy Institute (PPi). As institutions established to design and influence the development of public policy, think tanks are extremely important in the policy transfer process. During the 1980s and early 1990s there has been clear evidence that the ideas and policy proposals of the ASI and IEA were presented as the justification for new policies. More recently DEMOS and various 'electronic think tanks', such as Nexis, have been presented as the justification for new policies by both Conservative and Labour politicians (see Blackstone and Plowden 1988; Kandiah and Seldon 1996; Stone 1996).

As will be discussed in more detail in Chapter 5, another group who increasingly appear to be involved in the process of policy transfer, at both the voluntary and coercive levels, are national and international corporations. As Nellis stresses, corporations are connected to the process of policy transfer because of their involvement in lobbying governments, both directly and indirectly, for a particular policy or course of action which they favour. More importantly, this often occurs at a global level, so that over time numerous political systems adopt the same policies, based upon the advice and information provided by corporations advancing their particular product or service. Furthermore, as is well rehearsed within the globalization literature, corporations, particularly transnational corporations, gain a special influence in the process of semi-coercive policy transfer due to their power of investment. If a country depends upon a corporation for the welfare of a region or even the entire nation, it is likely that they will implement almost any policy or incentives to ensure that business is not taken elsewhere.

International governing organizations (IGOs) such as the Organization for Economic Co-operation and Development (OECD), the G-8, and the International Monetary Fund (IMF) are increasingly playing a role in the spread of ideas, programmes and institutions across the globe. These organizations are able to influence national and locally based policy makers because they have the power to affect the conditions attached to international loans. Moreover, institutions like the G-8 and the OECD have the power to develop policies member states agree to implement. Furthermore, IGOs are increasingly using conferences and reports to spread information, ideas and even policies not just to member states but around the entire globe. So, for example, the OECD actually states that it:

> groups 29 member countries in an organisation that, most importantly, provides governments a setting in which to discuss, develop and perfect economic and social policy. They compare experiences, seek answers to common problems and work to co-ordinate domestic and international policies that . . . must form a web of even practice across nations . . . Much of the [OECD] research and analysis is published [and available to everyone and every nation].
>
> (OECD)

In addition to IGOs, over the past fifty years international non-governmental organizations (NGOs) have dramatically increased their influence over global public policy. While their level of influence varies across countries and policy areas there is no denying that through their ability to spread ideas and information on an international level they are beginning to shape the face of global public and social policies. As Gordenker and Weiss (1996: 17–18) put it:

> Nongovernmental organisations (NGOs) have in increasing numbers injected unexpected voices into international discourse about numerous problems of global scope. Especially during the last 20 years . . . interests have become active in political work once reserved for representatives of states . . . In their own ways, NGOs . . . grope . . . towards a modicum of 'global governance' . . . NGOs have now become an integral part of the process of setting agendas . . . and in carrying the results not only to governments but to other NGOs and individuals.

A number of other points are worth making here. First, these categories are not mutually exclusive; for example, consultants may well act as policy entrepreneurs, while policy entrepreneurs may operate through think tanks. Second, as will be demonstrated by the case studies within this volume, in any specific case of transfer more than one category of actor is almost certain to be involved. Third, involvement in the policy-making and policy-transfer processes is often facilitated through participation in a national or international policy network. Fourth, participation is not necessarily equated with influence. Fifth, different instances of policy transfer will involve different combinations of actors who will have different motivations for becoming involved in the process. Finally, different actors have different influence in the process and this will vary across time and across different cases of transfer; nevertheless there may be patterns. So, certain groups of actors are consistently influential across both time and space, even if they are not involved in any specific network. Other groups will be more or less influential depending upon the issue in question and their position within the policy-making cycle. For example, depending upon the structure of the political system some actors, such as the President of the United States or Cabinet Ministers in Britain, might be extremely influential at the agenda-setting stage, but much less influential at the policy formulation or implementation stages. At the same time, other actors, such as Congressmen and individual 'street level' bureaucrats may be more important at the formulation or implementation stages of the policy-making process than the President or Cabinet members.

The role of networks in the policy transfer process

As hinted at above, in order to influence policy decisions, individuals and groups must gain access to the government's decision-making process. Moreover, in this struggle not all interests have equal access to the decision-making process. Rather, institutionalized relationships develop between government officials and broader societal interests within a given policy domain (for good overviews see Marsh and Rhodes 1992; Marsh 1998; Marsh and Smith 2000). The actors involved within these policy domains tend to enjoy close, continual, and often privileged access to key government officials. These formalized contacts exist as national and international networks. Such networks can clearly be one of the primary mechanisms for the spread of information among various actors on a global scale. More importantly, such networks can play a crucial role in placing information on the governing agenda.

Associated with, but distinct from, policy networks are advocacy coalitions. While networks focus on groups and individuals interacting within a policy domain, advocacy coalitions refer to a small number of groups which enter into strategic alliances based upon deeply shared values or 'fundamental ideological principles'. It is these shared beliefs and values that drive actors to work together both within and across national boundaries in the promotion of specific policies within a given policy subsystem. These coalitions are important in the development and spread of policies and programmes and, thus, must be acknowledged within any developing model of policy transfer. As with networks the membership of advocacy coalitions is diverse, comprising 'actors from a variety of public and private institutions at all levels of government who share a set of basic beliefs and who seek to manipulate government to achieve these goals over time' (Sabatier and Jenkins-Smith 1993: 5). More importantly for the process of policy transfer, advocacy coalitions are 'involved in policy formulation and implementation, as well as . . . in the generation, dissemination and evaluation of policy ideas' (Sabatier 1987: 663).

Epistemic communities also play a role in the process of policy transfer. Like policy networks and advocacy coalitions, epistemic communities are also collections of groups and individuals involved in the development and promotion of public policies within a given policy domain. What distinguishes these communities from other categories of networks is that they form around a system of shared knowledge and operate through policy regimes. Such knowledge is largely based on quantitative data supplied by professional organizations or policy specialists. This knowledge is then moulded into 'consensual knowledge', or commonly accepted cause and effect propositions, which defines the nature of policy problems and shapes the responses available to government (Haas 1990). Thus, policy making is about the use of knowledge to define political interests and to refine the ideological basis of policy proposals. Like advocacy coalitions, epistemic communities may 'share a common causal model and set of beliefs' but, unlike advocacy coalitions, this is more akin to a community of scientists 'like biologists' than to groups bound together by ideological principles. Epistemic communities not only help transfer ideas and policies around the globe but when there is more than one epistemic community in a policy environment they can be seen to behave like 'rival groups of scientists', in that the ultimate test of their 'version of the truth' is the adoption of their prognoses by the users of knowledge (Haas 1990: 42). Thus, it is in the interest of the epistemic community to ensure that the maximum number of political actors and systems adopt their policies and proposals.

It should be pointed out that while the policy transfer literature has only begun to integrate the role of the different types of networks presented here, as this volume demonstrates, they have clearly had an important influence in the transfer of policies, programmes and institutions from the United States to the United Kingdom. In fact, as Hulme argues in Chapter 4, without the influence of networks it is doubtful that the British higher education system would look as it does today. Similarly, Nellis illustrates that the course followed by, and outcomes of, policy transfer are often determined by the interaction of two or more networks working within the same policy domain.

What is transferred?

While almost anything can be transferred from one political system to another, depending upon the issue or situation involved, it is possible to identify six general categories: policy goals, content and instruments; programmes; institutions; ideologies; ideas and attitudes; and negative lessons.

While most of these categories are self-explanatory it is worth stressing a few of the distinctions made here. First, in most conceptions of the policy-making and policy transfer processes, programmes and policies are conflated into a single category. This is clearly misguided given that distinctions do exist between the two. More specifically, policies are generally seen as broad statements of intention which represent the direction in which policy makers wish to go. Programmes on the other hand are the specific means or course of action used to implement policies. Or, as the fathers of implementation studies Pressman and Wildavsky (1973: xxii–xxiii) put it: 'The word "program" . . . can be conceived of as a system in which each element is dependent on the other . . . Policies imply theories . . . Policies become programs when, by authoritative action, the initial conditions are created.' Thus, it should be clear that each policy can have multiple programmes, while a programme is a complete course of action in and of itself. So, in the process of policy transfer it is more likely that policy makers will transfer a programme than an entire policy. Equally, while policy makers might not be able to transfer an entire policy or programme they can, and do, transfer the goals, instruments and even content of particular policies and programmes from one political system to another.

The institutions used to implement policy can also be transferred, although this is generally not as straightforward, or easy, as the transfer of policies. So, it will be demonstrated in Chapter 2 that the Thatcher government developed the British Child Support Agency (CSA) based upon their knowledge of the American Child Support Enforcement System (CSES), particularly Wisconsin's Child Support Agency, and to a lesser extent Australia's CSA.

While the transfer of a programme or institution may not be possible, actors often attempt to transfer the ideologies and attitudes underlying a programme or institution from one system to another. Often this type of transfer is used to shift the political climate or to win a political battle. Thus, it will be demonstrated in Chapters 2 and 3 that one of the key reasons the Conservative governments of the 1980s and 1990s turned to the United States was that they were constantly trying to instil the attitudes underpinning American social policies into the British political and social systems. Moreover, during the past twenty years governments around the world, including the current Blair government (to a certain extent) have been actively borrowing the ideological rhetoric emerging from the American New Right in relation to welfare reform. This is particularly true in terms of the New Right's ideological rhetoric in relation to 'welfare dependency'; the need to 'enforce' obligations upon 'lazy' welfare 'scroungers'; and the growing use of concepts such as 'rights and responsibilities' and 'duties' (see Murray 1984; Mead 1986, 1997; Katz 1989; Pierson 1994, 1996).

Before moving on it is necessary to clarify what is meant by negative lessons. When drawing negative lessons policy makers explicitly decide to leave aspects of a foreign policy out of the transferred model or deliberately implement a borrowed model differently. For example, the Social Security Select Committee recently argued that while the United Kingdom could learn a great deal from American welfare reform programmes, particularly the Wisconsin W-2 model, they regarded Wisconsin's programme toward lone parents as being inappropriate for the UK. Specifically they argued that:

> Despite . . . differences in society and welfare systems, the American reforms raised a number of themes and issues that need to be addressed as the Government embarks on welfare reform in the United Kingdom . . . We believe that the British social security system should be more closely tailored to work requirements for claimants. We would not wish to see anything approaching Wisconsin's requirements for lone parents with young babies to work; any requirement involving under school age children seems counter-productive and possibly harmful to families.
>
> (SSSC 1998: 6–7)

From where are lessons drawn?

While this book is primarily concerned with international policy transfer between Britain and the United States, when developing a model for analysing the process of policy transfer it is necessary to identify all the levels of governance to which actors can, and do, look for lessons. When engaging in policy transfer policy makers can look to three levels of governance: the international level; the national level; and the local level.

Within a nation actors engaging in policy transfer can, and do, draw lessons from other political systems or units within their own country. This is particularly useful, and likely, if a nation's constitutional structures create a series of similar sub-national units of government. This process is further enhanced when there exists a relatively harmonious political culture across the nation. It should be stressed that not only can subnational units of government draw lessons from each other, but the national or federal government can also draw lessons from lower levels of government, while lower level of government can draw on the national level.

As will be illustrated more thoroughly in Chapter 4, policy transfer can also occur within unitary systems. As Rose (1991: 18) argues: 'In a unitary state . . . there is an explicit hierarchy of authority . . . ideas [move] up and down this hierarchy.' Not only do ideas move up and down an explicit hierarchy but it is common for local units of government to transfer ideas among themselves.

This book will also demonstrate that although constraints exist, it is common for policy makers and other political actors to transfer policies from one nation to another. When drawing lessons from other nations actors are not limited to looking at national governments but can look to other subnational levels and units of government within that nation.

Lessons can also be drawn, or forced upon a political system, from the international level. As discussed earlier, one of the primary reasons international organizations and institutions can perform this function is that they have the financial resources to force many nations to 'accept' given policies or programmes. In a less ominous way, they are also able to facilitate the process of policy transfer because they often act as stores of information to be drawn upon by national-based political systems and actors. More importantly, they bring together policy makers from various polities who are then able to share ideas and policy proposals.

Finally, as Hulme discusses in Chapter 4, in addition to other locations, policy makers can, and do, look to both their own past and to the global past. Searching the past has the advantage of saving resources, both political and economic, associated with transferring lessons from 'foreign' political systems. However, while searching the past has the advantage of saving time and resources it involves subjective evaluation, for while history is constant it is open to many interpretations. Indeed, when drawing lessons actors often do not understand the past or its relation to the present, clearly increasing the possibility that the lesson transferred from the past will fail to achieve the desired outcome.

Degrees of transfer

Policy transfer is not an all-or-nothing process. While any particular case of transfer may involve a combination of processes and agents, there are basically four different gradations or degrees of transfer: copying, which involves direct and complete transfer; emulation, which involves transfer of the ideas behind, but not the details of, the policy or programme; combinations, which involve mixtures of several different policies or programmes; and inspiration, where policy in another jurisdiction may inspire a policy change, but where the final outcome bears relatively little relationship or similarity to the original (see also Rose 1993).

Facilitators of, and restrictions on, policy transfer

When applying a model of policy transfer academics and researchers must not only consider the core elements of the typology but they must also consider what factors can facilitate or restrict the process (recalling that each facilitator can also act as a restriction given a different set of circumstances). These factors help explain why some policies are transferred while others are not and why policies are transferred from some systems rather than others. While the inherent characteristics of a society's political, cultural and social structures will themselves constrain or facilitate the ability of policy makers to engage successfully in policy transfer, basically there are seven broad categories to consider: policy complexity; interactive effects; institutional constraints; structural constraints; feasibility constraints; past relationships; and language constraints.

The first possible set of factors acting upon an agent's ability to engage in policy transfer involves questions of policy complexity. Specifically, it is likely that the more complex a policy or programme is, the harder it will be to transfer. While complexity can refer to almost any factor associated with a policy or programme, some of the more common would be the number of goals being addressed; the policy's dependence upon other factors, political, social and economic; the degree to which it is, or will be, associated with, or dependent upon, other policies; or even the degree to which policy makers can predict possible side effects, for the fewer the side effects, the less complex policy makers may perceive the policy as being. Thus, it is generally in the interest of the transferring agent to make the policy or programme desired seem as simple as possible, or to break it into its component parts and advocate the transfer of only what is necessary.

Institutional and structural factors will also influence the decision to engage in policy transfer. If the institutional structures of two systems are too dissimilar, the possibilities of transfer are severely restricted. In contrast, some structures can greatly facilitate transfer. So, in the transfer of policies from the United States to Britain the unitary structure of the British political system, when combined with the size of the government's majority during much of the 1980s and 1990s, greatly enhanced its ability to borrow from the US.

More directly, the structure and procedures found within individual government departments and agencies can facilitate or restrict transfer. For example, departments and agencies with well-developed hierarchies and reporting procedures might find the process of policy transfer considerably easier than those without. This is because well-developed hierarchical structures and procedures can facilitate the movement of ideas onto the department's policy agenda. Conversely, these same hierarchies can act as a restraint to policy transfer as juniors must submit proposals and ideas to managers who can prevent the information from ever reaching the policy agenda. Along these same lines, policy transfer is more likely to develop in departments where an open and harmonious culture has developed. Not only will this encourage the development of new ideas and ways of viewing problems but when there is a positive working relationship between Ministers and senior civil servants both sides are more likely to listen to the advice being provided by the other.

The structures of existing legislation and policies also shape the boundaries of policy transfer. For example, there is little doubt that the welfare-to-work system the Blair government inherited from the previous Conservative governments restricted its ability to alter existing programmes and what it perceived as viable alternatives. Here, the structure of the Conservative welfare-to-work system shaped how the new Labour elected representatives, officials and administrators perceived its problems, the acceptable 'solutions' to these problems, and the acceptable modifications. This fact is clearly expressed in the 1998 *United Kingdom Employment Action Plan*. Through the entire *Action Plan* the government relates its intention to utilize many of the welfare-to-work measures established by the Thatcher and Major governments in its own efforts to reform the welfare state (DfEE 1998b).[7]

The relationship between two political systems can itself enhance or deter agents from engaging in transfer. Past or existing relationships can either facilitate or prevent agents from looking to the past or an existing political system for solutions. Even within a federal system, sub-units which have a traditionally antagonistic relationship with the central government, or have a political system dominated by individuals who are ideologically antagonistic to that of the national government or even other state governments, will rarely have their policies or ideas accepted or even examined. On the other hand, systems having a tradition of harmonious relationships both within and across national boundaries will have established the lines of communication necessary for 'effective' policy transfer and may thus act as a model more often than other systems. These generalizations also hold true for policy transfer of a more coercive nature. Under these conditions political systems having good relationships with the imposing institution, particularly international institutions, are less likely to attempt to change the policy at the implementation stage or through the delegation of responsibilities to subnational political institutions than countries having antagonistic relationships with the transferring institution.

The political, bureaucratic, technological and economic resource similarities between systems also influence where actors look for policies, and what policies are, or are not, transferred. In this sense, political ideology plays an important, if not dominant, role in determining where actors look for policies and what policies they accept and reject. As will be demonstrated throughout this volume, the neo-liberal ideology of the American and British governments inclined the Thatcher and Major governments to look towards American programmes in the development of the British equivalents. Equally, the Blair government has continued this affinity with the United States not only because of Labour's 'shift to the right' and the advent of 'Third Way' politics, but also because of the ideological and political similarities between Bill Clinton and Tony Blair.

Closely associated with political ideologies are societal values, or cultural proximity. When engaging in policy transfer agents are constrained by the prevailing values of both other political actors and society more generally. If the prevailing values of two societies or political systems are similar the possibilities of transfer are greatly enhanced. At the same time, transfer is severely restricted when values are too dissimilar. Thus, one of the key reasons the Thatcher government looked to the US for ideas on coping with the problem of lone and absent parents was that it perceived an affinity between the cultures of the two countries which it believed would permit US solutions to be imported into Britain.

Obviously, even desirable programmes will not be transferred if implementation is beyond a nation's technological abilities. However, even when there are differences, if the technologies themselves can be transferred there is an increased possibility that policies and programmes relying upon these technologies will be transferred. For example, Chapter 5 will clearly demonstrate that the ability of Britain to adopt American technological developments in the area of criminal policy greatly enhanced the attractiveness of the American electronic monitoring programme. Moreover, this chapter also demonstrates that until the American 'tagging' technology was readily available, even though the government was interested in the American programme of electronic monitoring of criminals, they were not able, or willing, to transfer the policy to Britain.

Associated with technological restrictions are fiscal resource restraints. As Rose (1993: 96) argues: 'Money matters, for programs vary greatly in what they cost, and it is hard to apply lessons learned from programs beyond the fiscal means of a public agency.' Hence, it is often a combination of economic and technological restrictions which prevents developing nations from adopting Western programmes and policies, not the lack of political desire or knowledge.

The ability to engage in policy transfer will also be affected by the skills resources available to policy makers. Not only are skills necessary to engage in policy transfer but many policies and programmes call on a very specific set of skills being present. Thus, it is clear that one of the reasons the CSA failed to meet the performance targets set for it by the government was that its staff did not have the skills necessary to perform the tasks required of them during the first year the Agency was operational (Craig *et al.* 1996). Similarly, while it might be very desirable to operate an American-style management-information computer system very few developing countries have either the financial, technological, or personnel resources available, despite the pressure they may be receiving from international aid agencies to implement such systems.

Obviously, past policies constrain what can be transferred, what agents look for, and which agents engage in policy transfer. For example, in the United States, even though the Personal Responsibility and Work Opportunity Act of 1996 (PRWOA) supposedly 'ended welfare as we know it', Congress and the Clinton administration were constrained by the pre-existing structures established by the Work Incentive Program (WIN); the welfare-to-work programmes initiated in response to the 1981 Omnibus Budget Reconciliation Act (OBRA); the job search programmes initiated in the 1982 Tax Equity and Fiscal Responsibility Act (TEFRA); and the 1988 Family Support Act (FSA). Overall, these programmes were so influential in the development of the 1996 Act that while there were some major reforms, such as the imposition of a five-year lifetime limit placed upon the receipt of Temporary Assistance to Needy Families (TANF) (the successor programme to AFDC), and a shift in the funding arrangements from a matching categorical grant to a discretionary block grant, the programmes contained within the legislation were little more than incremental developments of previous programmes (US Government 1996).

Finally, although perhaps not a major constraint on policy transfer, the role of language similarities is not negligible. In the development of policies the ability to access documentation and discuss policies directly with individuals in a foreign system enhances the attractiveness of some systems over others.

However, with a shared language, there is a tendency to assume that actors understand the meanings contained within the language and implementation of policies and programmes. The assumption that understanding accompanies language similarities can often help account for why policies which appear to be working in one system fail when implemented into another. This often happens when language similarities mask cultural or political differences upon which success in the originating system depend.

Sources of information

Having presented the basic model of analysis that will appear within this volume it is worth illustrating some of the sources that can be used by agents of change in their search for 'foreign' models and ideas. Not only are these the primary sources used to garner information on foreign systems but they were also the primary means the contributors to this volume used in collecting their information. Another reason it is worth mentioning some of the mechanisms used by policy makers engaging in policy transfer is that researchers generally must provide a preponderance of evidence that transfer actually occurred, for seldom will there be a single 'empirical' way to prove that policy transfer was involved, or if it was involved, how important it was. This is true even if a Minister or senior civil servant 'claims' that transfer was involved, for it is often in their interest to do so, even though it might not be the case.

This noted, some of the more readily available sources used by policy makers engaging in policy transfer and researchers looking for evidence of it are the media; the internet; reports and studies; physical contact; and government records. While these sources are available to all agents of change, it should be stressed that different agents will rely upon different sources of information depending upon their position and role in the policy-making and policy transfer processes.

Media

While there are numerous means through which agents of change learn about policies or programmes in other political systems, one of the most common is through the mass media, particularly newspapers and magazines. By examining the content of newspapers and magazines it is possible to begin establishing what information was widely available to agents of change during the time period under examination. For example, in Chapter 5, Nellis clearly demonstrates that the major national newspapers in Britain were aware of American 'tagging' programmes and were influential in the government's decision both to delay and then to develop the British electronic monitoring programme. Likewise, in Chapter 4, Hulme demonstrates that at a minimum the *Guardian* was aware of, and discussing, the American influence on the development of British higher education during the late 1980s and early 1990s.

As with newspapers, magazines can help bring a foreign system to the attention of policy makers and academics. For example, each week the *Economist* publishes OECD data. This clearly helps to spread OECD data around the globe to policy makers interested in transferring particular policies or programmes. Interestingly for the process of semi-coercive policy transfer, often the data presented in the *Economist* instils a sense of dread among policy makers who are afraid of falling behind their major competitors or simply want to be considered legitimate actors on the world stage. On the opposite side, in Chapter 5 Nellis documents several instances of where the *New Statesman and Society* actually 'castigated the Home Office for looking across the Atlantic' for penal inspiration.

Television also provides information on foreign systems. For example, in the transfer of American welfare-to-work programmes to Britain, British policy makers were often exposed to American welfare-to-work programmes through a variety of television documentaries. Dolowitz (1998) demonstrated that one of the more influential of these occurred on 7 April 1986, when BBC's *Panorama* programme analysed American welfare-to-work programmes. Once this programme was broadcast policy makers including the Prime Minister herself began referring to both the programme and the American welfare-to-work system.

Radio, particularly news and current affairs programmes, provides politicians, academics and the general public with considerable information on foreign models. For example, in the reform of the welfare state both the Conservative and Labour governments have benefited from the research conducted by the BBC's *Analysis* programme. For example, on both 16 October 1997 and 26 March 1998, *Analysis* broadcast programmes which thoroughly reviewed the American welfare-to-work system and talked to some of the key players involved in promoting, analysing and developing its reforms, including Jean Rogers, the Director of Wisconsin's welfare-to-work programme; Lawrence Mead, one of the key promoters of welfare-to-work programmes in both the US and the UK; and Robert Walker, one of the key British academics examining and promoting the American welfare-to-work systems for the UK.[8]

Internet

The internet is becoming an increasingly important source of information for individuals engaging in policy transfer. Not only can it provide direct access to most of the world's governments, pressure groups, media outlets etc., but it also provides a means of directly accessing government documents. For example, almost every document published by the American government, not considered classified, is placed on the internet within 24 hours of its release. Similarly, in Britain most government departments, including Parliament, place their primary documents and press releases on the internet the day they are published in print. Prime Minister Tony Blair probably captured the essence of the internet's importance to policy transfer when speaking to the Nexus/*Guardian* conference:

Let me also applaud the energy and intellect of the people who make up Nexus, Britain's first virtual think-tank. Nexus is not just frighteningly youthful: it is made up of people who are free from cynicism without being naive, striving for new insights without forgetting old ones. Nexus has a crucial role in sustaining the momentum of progressive politics, not just in opposition but in Government too.

(Blair 1997)

Perhaps the most telling indication of the internet's perceived importance is the Blair government's declared intent to have every school in the country internet-accessible within the life of the existing Parliament.

Reports and studies

In the process of policy transfer agents of change often commission reports and studies. These reports are a prime source of information on other systems. Additionally, the existence of these reports is critical for demonstrating both knowledge and interest in other systems. For example, since coming to power, the Blair government has commissioned numerous reports on the American welfare-to-work system, including reports on workfare, the minimum wage and the Earned Income Tax Credit. In fact, in the second of the three-volume *Modernisation of Britain's Tax and Benefit System*, Martin Taylor acknowledged the importance of American ideas and programmes in the development of the British Working Families Tax Credit (WFTC). As Taylor stated: 'at Gordon Brown's request, [I] looked at what lessons could be learned from the experience of the Earned Income Tax Credit (EITC) in the US' (1998: 8).

Physical meetings

In addition to the media and the issuing of reports, physical meetings provide ample evidence that agents of change were provided with information on policies and programmes in operation elsewhere. These contacts can be used as an inspiration for change, the justification needed to go ahead with policies and programmes already developed, or even as the basis of the development of new policies, programmes, institutions, etc. For example, shortly after the Labour government came to power, the entire Social Security Select Committee took an extensive 'study' visit to the US to examine both federal and several state welfare-to-work and workfare programmes. In fact, in their report on the visit, the Select Committee advised the government to adopt many of the American strategies and programmes (SSSC 1998).

One of the first places agents of change can come into contact with individuals knowledgeable about the functioning of other systems is at conferences, particularly conferences organized to discuss a particular topic or area. At conferences agents are exposed to new ideas and individuals developing, working on and researching a variety of models. Often this can act as the inspiration for policy transfer. So, as will be discussed in Chapter 4, it has been documented that one of the key reasons the Thatcher government developed the Child Support Agency (CSA) was that one of her key advisers, David Willetts, met Irwin Garfinkel at a Paris conference where they discussed the American Child Support Enforcement System (CSES).

Besides the contacts made at conferences, official and unofficial visits to other political systems provide further evidence of policy transfer. This is particularly important if the visits occurred before the development of the policy in question. So, in Chapter 5 Nellis documents that one of the interesting features of electronic monitoring was the way different countries used the information they gathered from their visits to the United States. For example, he shows that representatives from the UK, Sweden and the Netherlands visited the United States to examine how electronic monitoring operated; that each team was given access to the same information and experiences; and that each team visited the same institutions at the same time. However, the conclusions drawn by each nation were extremely different, leading to different policy outcomes in each country.

In a similar vein, Hulme documents how policy makers used visits to the United States, France, Germany, Holland, Australia and New Zealand to push for education reforms that would increase the number of students in British higher education to a level similar to that of the United States. Interestingly, they argued that to do otherwise 'would weaken the basis of national competitiveness'.

How can we demonstrate policy transfer?

While the above sources illustrate the primary level and paths of information available to different agents they do not confirm that policy makers utilized this information in the development of policies. While an empirical and methodological question, there are several techniques which can be used to help demonstrate that actors were aware of programmes operating elsewhere, were interested in them, and utilized them in the development of policies, programmes and institutions. In the case studies presented within the remainder of this book the primary sources used to demonstrate the existence of policy transfer between the United States and Britain were official references to media reports; studies commissioned by the government; official references to studies published by independent groups and organizations; government records; and personal interviews.

Government statements

Of the sources of information mentioned above, official government statements in written records and interviews provide the most direct evidence that transfer has occurred.[9] So, for example, as will be demonstrated in Chapter 2, there is clear evidence within Parliamentary records that the American, Wisconsin and Australian child support enforcement systems were highly influential in the development of the British CSA. Similarly, Nellis uses government records to establish that the Conservative government used the American 'tagging' system to develop the British system of electronic monitoring.

Demonstrating that there was information available, and that agents of transfer were aware of it, is a key aspect of any analysis of policy transfer because just showing that policies look alike is not evidence of transfer. As this chapter has illustrated, the first step in demonstrating that policies and programmes were the result of policy transfer is to begin with a clear understanding of the phenomenon under study. Once the object of transfer has been clarified, the agent or agents of transfer need to be established. It is essential to establish the agents of transfer because policy transfer must be a conscious process, whether this is undertaken voluntarily or as the result of coercion. Once the object and agent of transfer have been established, evidence of policy transfer must be established. Clearly, evidence will depend upon both the nature of the political system and the object being transferred. For example, evidence of idea or attitude transfer will generally depend more on interview data and the subjective interpretations of the recipient. On the other hand, support for the transfer of a programme or institution will require more physical evidence.

Policy transfer and policy failure

Before concluding this chapter it is important to stress that the research presented in this volume clearly suggests that although there is increasing evidence of policy transfer, not all, or even most, transfer is successful. Thus it is important to examine why transfer is unsuccessful; that is to identify which factors are related to successful or unsuccessful transfer. Obviously, when looking at the role of policy transfer in the failure of a particular policy, programme or institution there is a problem with establishing what is meant by 'success' or 'failure' (Bovens and 'tHart 1996). However, as will become clear within the case studies, two possible definitions of success are the extent to which a transferred policy achieves the stated aims set by the government when engaging in transfer; and whether the policy, programme or institution was seen as a success by the key actors involved in the process.

In cases of lesson drawing at least, governments borrow policies, programmes and institutions from other jurisdictions with the expectation that this transfer will lead to 'success', even if this success is of a symbolic nature. In these cases the underlying assumption is that policies which have been 'successful' in one political system will be successful in another. However, this clearly is not the case. In particular, the research presented in this volume suggests that in addition to the causes of failure already mentioned, resulting from the process of policy transfer itself, there are at least three other factors which have a significant effect on policy failure. First, the borrowing system may have insufficient information about the policy/institution and how it operates in the originating system – a process referred to as unknowledgable transfer in Chapter 2. Second, although transfer has occurred, crucial elements of what made the policy or institutional structure a success in the originating country may not be transferred, leading to failure – a process referred to as incomplete transfer in Chapter 2. Third, as discussed throughout the book, insufficient attention may be paid to the differences between the economic, social, political and ideological contexts in the transferring and borrowing systems – a process referred to as inappropriate transfer in Chapter 2.

To take one example, at present it appears that the Blair government's attempts to reform the existing Conservative workfare system are likely to encounter serious problems. Although they have consciously set out to draw lessons from the United States, they have concentrated on relatively small aspects of the entire system and only a few of the more publicized state systems. This is clearly reflected in the Social Security Select Committee's Second Report, *Lessons from the United States of America* (SSSC 1998). The key point is that if the government extended its examination of the 'American' welfare-to-work system to include states such as Utah or Oregon, it is likely that they would learn some of the drawbacks of the system they appear to be implementing. Moreover, if they examined the federal welfare system over time they would probably realize that the overall 'success' of the system relies less upon any individual policy or programme than on a strong economy and a willingness to let some of the poorest of the poor fall through the welfare safety net.

Policy transfer and the policy-making process

Before moving into the case studies it is worth discussing how policy transfer can enhance our understanding of the overall policy-making process. However, prior to doing this, let me stress that policy makers can engage in transfer for different purposes and at different stages of the policy-making process. For example, while not an exhaustive list it should be clear that some of the key motives for engaging in transfer are to set the systemic and/or institutional agendas; solve problems; appear to be acting upon a problem (or to make a symbolic gesture towards 'solving' the problem); alter the course of existing policies, programmes or 'rules of the game'; harmonize one system with other nations or the international system; penetrate another system; or simply to learn what is going on outside an indigenous situation or system.

Policy transfer clearly aids our understanding of the policy-making process. Part of this is that policy transfer helps us avoid a truncated view of policy making by extending the focus of policy analysis, making clear the importance of foreign models within the process. This point is easily illustrated if we consider the question of policy failure. When traditional policy analysts declare a programme a 'failure', they often neglect to recognize that the policy's origins influence its chances of 'failure' or 'success'. Certainly, when a programme originates from the process of policy transfer, subsequent problems may have little to do with the programme in and of itself. Rather, if it is used within the borrowing system in a way not intended in the original model, problems will almost inevitably emerge. At the same time, the 'success' of the programme in the originating system may depend upon cultural or institutional factors which were either ignored or not understood by the borrowing system, so inappropriate lessons may have been drawn.

In addition to helping policy analysis move beyond single country perspectives, policy transfer can also illuminate traditional policy-making studies which split the process into anywhere between five and nine stages. By way of illustration, Hogwood and Gunn (1984), identify nine stages in the policy-making cycle: agenda setting (deciding to decide); issue filtration (deciding how to decide); issue definition; forecasting; setting objectives; option analysis; policy implementation, monitoring and control; evaluation and review; and policy maintenance, succession and termination. Policy transfer clearly increases our understanding of several of these stages.

The agenda-setting stage involves the identification of problems or opportunities which require action. However, as Hogwood and Gunn (1984: 7) note: 'One of the least explored aspects of real-life policy-making in Britain is how certain issues get on political agendas for discussion and action while others do not.' Because the contributors to this volume use the framework presented within this chapter, this problem is avoided. For example, by using policy transfer as a dependent variable, Chapters 2 and 3 identify a variety of factors ranging from economic considerations to ideological commitments which lead policy makers to place issues and policies on the political agenda.

As soon as there is a recognition that a new way of doing things is needed, policy makers must begin to define the problem and decide how to deal with the issue. More specifically, Hogwood and Gunn argue that policy makers must consider whether a problem 'should be left to normal political and administrative process or should be selected for more fundamental and objective analysis' (p. 8). Policy transfer sheds light on both the issue filtration and issue definition stages of the policy process. For example, it is reasonable to assume that, in the absence of an acceptable alternative already existing within the political system, policy makers will engage in some sort of search. Before engaging in this search policy makers will, by definition, have to attach a meaning to the issue which makes another political system's policy or programme both acceptable and attractive.

A policy transfer model can also expand our understanding of the option analysis stage of policy development. It is reasonable to assume that once a 'foreign' policy has been perceived as necessary and desirable there will be some sort of contact between the two systems in which information is exchanged. This information must then be evaluated, assessing what changes, if any, would be needed to implement it in the borrowing system. It is at this stage that decision makers take the initial decision either to copy, emulate or mix policies found elsewhere in the development of domestic policy solutions. This stage can also inspire policy makers, who deem a programme in operation elsewhere inappropriate to their existing situation. In this situation they may decide to adapt an indigenous policy to address the situation.

What this demonstrates is that if researchers fail to analyse the role of 'foreign' policies and programmes in the development of indigenous policies and programmes many of the options open to, and used by, policy makers will be overlooked, with the consequence that analysts will fail fully to appreciate the complexities of the policy outcome and the decision-making process.

A policy transfer focus can also help explain the processes of policy evaluation and reformation. In using borrowed policies and programmes policy makers should examine the impact of policies on the original system. Even if they do not examine the 'impact' of borrowed policies, policy makers will most likely adapt the programme during the process of implementation, in light of new information on the programme's impact and as they continue to learn more about policies and programmes in operation elsewhere.

Conclusion

As this brief review demonstrates, in order to understand policy transfer it is necessary to use the entire model presented above. It should be clear that it is not enough simply to see what is transferred; one must also consider the motivations involved. Moreover, the model, and particularly the continuum, demonstrate that generally it is not enough to examine transfer as if it were an all-or-nothing process. Rather, longitudinal studies are required to capture the shifting motivations involved. Moreover, it is also clear that policies borrowed from other political systems develop over time and that much of this development involves shifts between voluntary and coercive motivations, particularly when it becomes apparent that a chosen course of action is not working as policy makers had intended.

It should also be clear that in order to understand where a case falls within this model it is important to identify the key actors because different actors will have different motivations. For example, as a general rule it is probable that, when politicians or policy entrepreneurs institute the process, they will be doing it voluntarily. While it will seldom be a completely voluntary or rational process it will be less coercive than if other actors institute the process. The particular activity in question must also be understood before a full picture of the transfer process can be developed. For example, when aid agencies are making loans it is likely to involve coercive policy transfer. Yet at the same time, when these same organizations hold conferences or issue reports it is more likely to involve some form of voluntary policy transfer.

It should also be clear that different policies and programmes will naturally result from the involvement of different actors and motivations. Moreover, when policy transfer occurs it is likely to affect the motivations of the actors engaging in the process. For example, if policy transfer is undertaken during periods of social, political and economic stability within a nation such transfer is likely to be voluntary. However, if there is some form of political crisis, then transfer is likely to have some coercive elements. Equally, if there is some form of 'global' crisis, such as the economic downturn during the early 1990s, actors are more likely to feel pressure to engage in transfer than when the global political and economic situation appears to be stable.

The model presented within this chapter treats policy transfer as essentially a dependent variable; as something we need to explain. As such, the questions the model highlights concern either the characteristics of the transfer or the reasons for the transfer. So, it is necessary to ask two questions about the characteristics of the transfer: what was transferred; and what degree of transfer occurred? At the same time, this chapter has focused on three questions about the reasons for transfer: who transfers policy; why is policy transferred; and what factors constrain or facilitate policy transfer? As the case studies presented within this volume demonstrate and research certainly supports, policy transfer is a useful explanatory variable. However, this volume clearly does not suggest that policy transfer is the sole explanation of any, let alone most, policy development. Given these observations, it should be obvious that it was necessary to advance a model for analysing the process of transfer before using the concept to explore the development of various areas of British social policy. Thus, this chapter developed the model that will be used within the remainder of this book to frame individual contributors' analysis of British social policy.

2

Welfare: the Child Support Agency

David P. Dolowitz

In late 1990 the Thatcher government published a two-volume White Paper, *Children Come First: The Government's Proposals on the Maintenance of Children* (DSS 1990), announcing its intention to establish a Child Support Agency. The White Paper's proposals were given effect in the 1991 Child Support Act which established the structure and general functions of the Child Support Agency, which began operating in April 1993.

Most of the debate surrounding the British Child Support Agency (CSA) since its establishment in 1993, and its subsequent reforms, including the 1995 Child Support Act and the Labour government's recent proposals in the Green Paper *Children First: A New Approach to Child Support* (DSS 1998a), have concentrated on the problems, or perceived problems, of implementation which the CSA has encountered. This debate has mainly focused upon issues such as the impact the Agency has had on the families ordered to pay maintenance contributions, regardless of their income, assets or existing financial responsibilities; the difficulty the Agency has faced in forcing women to help in paternity establishment; the negative effects of child support orders on the relationship between ex-partners and their children; the almost universally inaccurate assessment of support awards, based upon the assessment formula; the initial inability of the CSA to adjust child support orders to the existing circumstances of the parents, due to the Agency's remit to stick rigidly to the formula; and various administrative issues.

Unlike most of the existing literature, this chapter is not directly concerned with identifying the problems the Agency has experienced over the past six years. Rather, it concentrates upon how the Agency was developed and how its development can help explain some of the reasons for its subsequent problems. More directly, the analysis presented here will show that the origins of the Agency are to be found in policy transfer from the United States and, to a lesser extent, Australia; and that inappropriate transfer from the US led to important implementation problems.

To establish both that there was transfer, and that this transfer led to the Agency's implementation problems, it is useful to break the analysis found within this chapter into four stages. First, it is important to identify what led actors to search for lessons from abroad. Second, it must be demonstrated that policy makers were aware of, and interested in, the American Child Support Enforcement System (CSES) and the Australian Child Support Agency. Third, it must be shown that policy makers used their knowledge of the American CSES and the Australian CSA in the development of the British CSA. Finally, it must be shown how this process led to the implementation problems experienced by the Agency. Thus the majority of this chapter will be organized around four questions. Why did the British government search abroad, particularly in the United States, for lessons in this area? Was there knowledge of, and interest in, the American CSES and Australian CSA prior to the development of the British CSA? What were the key structural elements of the Child Support Agency which were transferred from the American CSES? How did inappropriate policy transfer lead to implementation failure?

Why did the British government turn to the US for lessons?

There were four key reasons why the government decided to transfer the structure and functions of the Child Support Agency from the United States. First, the US and Britain were facing similar problems within their child support enforcement systems; second, the Reagan administration and the Thatcher government shared ideological values; third, the Thatcher government saw the Agency as a means of reducing the public sector borrowing requirement (PSBR); fourth, America's CSES had a long history of 'success'.

Similar problems

In the United States, the passage of the 1974 Social Service Amendments, the 1984 Child Support Enforcement Amendments and the 1988 Family Support Act (FSA) were each inspired by the perceived need to enhance the consistency and accountability of America's child support system.[10] These Acts were a response to the inability of court-determined support orders, with no state or federal guidelines or accountability, to produce similar child support awards, even for families in similar situations.[11] It was particularly distressing to policy makers that families who needed help the most were the least likely to receive it, as few of them could afford the lawyers' fees, court costs and delays involved in establishing maintenance awards.[12] As Garfinkel and Klawiter (1990: 156) argue:

> Until recently child support was a state and local matter . . . The establishment and enforcement of private child support was characterized by judicial discretion . . . How much non-resident parents were required to pay in child support varied dramatically from case to case. Families in similar circumstances were treated quite differently.

While these problems were less prevalent in Britain they underpinned the arguments presented in *Children Come First* to justify the development of the CSA. The White Paper (DSS 1990: i) argues:

> The present system of maintenance is unnecessarily fragmented, uncertain in its results, slow and ineffective. It is based largely on discretion. The system is operated through the . . . courts . . . and the . . . Department of Social Security. The cumulative effect is uncertainty and inconsistent decisions about how much maintenance should be paid.

Interestingly, in the context of this chapter's emphasis on policy failure resulting from policy transfer, the Labour government made similar arguments in *Children First*, even though the CSA had been operating for over six years and, as will be discussed below, had undergone numerous administrative and procedural changes. Specifically *Children First* argues that the existing system for the collection and assessment of child support 'is unpredictable and its complexity makes it difficult to understand and administer. Too often it can harm, rather than help, family relationships' (DSS 1998a: 7).

Prior to the passage of the 1974 Social Service Amendments, the US Census Bureau indicated that only 6 in 10 lone parents eligible for child support had been granted an award. Compounding this problem, it was discovered that there was a considerable variation in the receipt of child support maintenance awards depending upon the prior marital status of the lone parent. Thus, whereas almost 80 per cent of divorced parents had an award, less than 10 per cent of 'never-married' parents had one. Even when support orders had been granted they tended to be low and were rarely updated in line with inflation or changes in the income of the absent or resident parent. Most disturbingly, the Census Bureau discovered that, even when maintenance awards had been granted, less than half were paid in full, while a quarter went totally unpaid (Garfinkel *et al.* 1992, 1994).

One year before the passage of the Child Support Enforcement Amendments of 1984, the US Bureau of the Census (1986) released figures revealing that, even after the passage of the 1974 Amendments, little had changed. For example, of the nearly 9 million eligible families in 1983, only about 4 million were receiving child support.[13] Corbett *et al.* discovered that of these only 'half received the entire award, another quarter received partial payments, and one out of four received no support at all' (1988: 633). Even after the passage of the

1984 Child Support Enforcement Amendments, the situation continued to be problematic. The Census Bureau indicated that only 40 per cent of eligible mothers had child support awards. Even worse, Garfinkel *et al.* discovered that the 'average awards and payments declined by 25 percent in real terms between 1978 and 1985' (1994: 6). Furthermore, even after the 1984 Amendments and a dramatic improvement in the rate of paternity establishment only 30 per cent of unmarried lone parents were in receipt of a maintenance award. More troubling for policy makers, there was a continuing rise in the number of 'never-married' single parents relying upon the AFDC system, which had originally been designed to support women and children who had lost their husbands.

The shortcomings in the two previous Amendments led presidential and congressional policy makers to include Title I in the 1988 Family Support Act (FSA). Title I of the 1988 FSA implemented a national child support enforcement system based upon the uniform application of a state-developed formula to guarantee that absent parents were held responsible for maintaining their children, even after the dissolution of the marriage (for more information see US Government 1988: Title I).

In Britain similar trends were highlighted in *Children Come First*. Cm 1264 indicated that in 1989 70 per cent of families who had been awarded child support received nothing, or less than they were entitled to. According to the White Paper this situation had arisen because many absent parents refused to make any payments or had fallen into arrears. In addition, of the payments which fell into arrears only 5 per cent were fully recovered (DSS 1990). As in the United States this situation was compounded because many eligible families failed to claim child support in the first instance. More importantly, the fastest growing group of lone parents, unmarried single parents, were the least likely to be in receipt of a maintenance award.

As a result of the problems highlighted above, a significant proportion of single parent families in both the US and Britain were relying on the welfare system. In fact, one of the main arguments used to justify the 1988 FSA was the need to reduce dependency among single parent families caused by the lack of child support payments. As noted by Nichols-Casebolt and Garfinkel: 'Failure to secure economic support from the fathers in these cases contributes to the economic disadvantages faced by these mothers as well as the fiscal burden borne by the public.' In response the 'US Congress and state legislatures have enacted legislation designed to facilitate the establishment of paternity and child support awards' (1991: 83–4).

Once again these arguments are replicated in Britain. For example, Volume II of *Children Come First* begins: 'Lone parent families have become more dependent on social security benefits and have become less likely to receive maintenance' (DSS 1990: Volume II, p. i). Similarly, in a speech given in early 1990, Mrs Thatcher directly linked the need to develop the Child Support Agency to the growing reliance of single parents upon the welfare state, caused by the lack of financial support from absent parents: 'No father should be able to escape from his responsibility and that is why the government is looking at ways of . . . making the arrangement for recovering maintenance more effective' (cited in Graham and Knights 1994: 1).

As will be discussed below, the extent to which the system has failed to rectify the situation can be seen in *Children First*. In Cm 3992 the Labour government argued: 'the existing child support scheme does not deliver . . . for the 1.8 million children on Income Support or Family Credit for whom no maintenance is being paid' (DSS 1998a: 7).

Not only were the US and Britain facing similar problems in the lack of, and inconsistency in, the setting of child support maintenance awards but the dramatic rise in the number of single parent families within both the US and Britain was constantly being associated with the apparent 'dependence' of single parents upon the state for financial support. In itself this might not have been perceived as a problem by the general public. However, during the later part of the 1980s many on the political right began linking single parents' apparent dependence on welfare payments to a deliberate avoidance of entering the labour market. This undermined their privileged position in both the US and the UK so that they could be attacked and have programmes such as the CSA forced upon them. Thus, in the United States, the number of children living in single parent families rose from only 8 per cent in 1960 to almost 25 per cent by 1990. In fact, it has been estimated that over half of the children born during the late 1970s and 1980s will live in a single parent family before the age of 18. It was Congressional concern with the rise in dependency among these families which motivated Congress to include both Title I programmes and a mandate for every state to include Aid to Families with Dependent Children Parents (AFDC-UP) programme within the 1988 FSA. Briefly, the AFDC-UP programme was designed to provide welfare benefits to low-income two parent families as opposed to the AFDC programme which only targeted single parent families. Prior to the 1988 FSA, states were given the option of operating, but not required to operate, an AFDC-UP programme. For this reason only 27 states and the District of Columbia were operating AFDC-UP programmes prior to the passage of the 1988 FSA. Congress included the AFDC-UP provision because, during the Congressional Hearings leading to the passage of the Act, numerous witnesses testified that states which had eliminated their AFDC-UP programmes were discovering that families were breaking up in order to requalify for AFDC benefits. For example, in written testimony Cindy Haag, Director of the Office of Assistance Payments of the Utah Department of Social Services, states:

> Utah learned the hard way . . . what it is like when you don't serve two parent households . . . without the program in place, we heard . . . that families were breaking up. The mothers and the children were coming back on full AFDC . . . we were breaking up the families . . . We did a study and found that to be true.
>
> (US Government 1987a: 96)

This same pattern was repeated in Britain, though on a much smaller scale. However, given the size differences between the US and British populations, the increase in the number of single parents was proportionally similar to what was occurring in the United States. Specifically Craig *et al.* (1996: 107) found that 'Between 1971 and 1991 the number of lone parent families rose from 0.6 million to 1.3 million, the later containing 2.2 million children.' More important for the argument presented here, 'never-married' parents, who were statistically much more likely to depend upon welfare payments, comprised over one-third of these families. These trends were clearly noticed by the government prior to the development of the Agency. As noted in the Social Security Advisory Committee's *Seventh Report*:

> In the 1980s the number of lone parents has risen more rapidly than at any other time . . . Some two thirds of all lone parents receiving benefit receive income support. Of these, over half are divorced or separated and half have at least one child under five.
>
> (SSAC 1990: 44)

The Committee used these trends to justify the need to improve the British child support maintenance system. Specifically, the Committee argued that, while the number of lone parents claiming benefits was increasing, 'over the same period the amount of maintenance paid by non-custodial parents has been static . . . Many possible options are now being considered to resolve the problem of parents who default in paying maintenance' (p. 44).

Because both countries were facing similar circumstances, the ability to turn to a well-developed and tested system increased the attractiveness of the American child support enforcement system and, in particular, the Wisconsin system.

Similar ideology

The decision to transfer the Child Support Agency from the US CSES was also influenced by the ideological similarities between the Reagan and Thatcher administrations. One of the key ideological arguments underpinning the development of both the CSES in the US and the CSA in Britain was the belief that parents should take responsibility for their biological children, regardless of the marital situation.[14] In the United States these arguments were forcefully represented in the 1974 Social Service Amendments, the 1984 Child Support Enforcement Amendments and the 1988 FSA. In fact, the opening statement of the 1984 Child Support Enforcement Amendment defines their purpose so as: 'To . . . ensure . . . that all children in the United States who are in need of assistance in securing financial support from their parents will receive such assistance regardless of their circumstances' (US Government 1984: Introduction).

These sentiments were reiterated during the passage of the 1988 FSA. For instance, during testimony before the Senate Committee on Finance (US Government 1987a), Senator Thad Cochrin argued:

There is agreement on the importance of parental support for children
. . . we start by placing primary responsibility on parents to support their
children . . . The automatic wage withholding requirement in the Bill
makes a needed statement . . . that this nation expects fathers to help support [their] children.

(US Government 1987a: 6–7)

This same belief was apparent in Britain dating back to the 1986 Social
Security Act. Specifically, Sections 24–6 of the Act mandates that both men
and women were liable to maintain their children until they were 16 years old
(and in some instances 19 years old). This mandate was true even if the parents
had been divorced, separated or the child was illegitimate. The Thatcher government was so adamant about the responsibilities of parents for the maintenance of their offspring that they strengthened the wording of the 1986 Social
Security Act in the 1989 Social Security Act, in order to ensure young people
did not have recourse to state aid. Section 5 of the Act mandates that a father
was liable to maintain 'any children of whom he is the father', and that both
men and women were liable to maintain any children 'of whom the man or
the woman is the father or mother', regardless of their marital status or relationship (DSS 1989: Section 5). *Children Come First* repeats these sentiments in
its opening paragraph:

Every child has a right to care from his or her parents . . . Although events
may change the relationship between the parents . . . those events cannot
in any way change their responsibilities towards their children . . . The
payment of child maintenance is one crucial way in which parents fulfil
their responsibilities towards their children.

(DSS 1990: Foreword)

In addition to the shared belief that parents had a continuing responsibility for the welfare of their children, even after divorce or separation, Britain
and the US shared a tradition of 'family policy' avoidance. While the British
system of 'child benefit' is a form of family policy, successive British and American
governments have explicitly avoided comprehensive policies to encourage or
discourage family formation.[15] In both Britain and the United States the avoidance of an explicit family policy has been identified in terms of the overrid-
ing principle of 'the sanctity and "privacy of the family"' (Ginsburg 1992: 165).
However, while the Reagan and Thatcher administrations avoided an explicit
family policy, they both professed to support strong 'family values'. This combination of values helped attract the Thatcher government to the American
CSES because, while the CSES was not an explicit family policy, it could be sold
as increasing and protecting family values, even after the dissolution of the family.

Not only are these sentiments re-expressed within *Children First* but the
Green Paper directly criticizes the institutional and cultural framework established by the 1991 and 1995 Acts. *Children First* argues that 'all children have
a right to emotional and financial support from both parents, wherever they

live. Existing child support arrangements do not uphold this basic right' (DSS 1998a: 9). In fact, the report goes on to argue that not only could the CSA not handle its caseload but that: 'Parents on Income Support currently see no direct gain for their children from their involvement with the CSA' (p. 10).

The Thatcher government's strong attachment to the work ethic further attracted it to the American CSES. Briefly, the 1988 FSA was passed not only to ensure absent parents met their financial obligations to their children, but also to require them to support their children through work. In the words of the Act's primary sponsor, Senator Moynihan:

> The primary responsibility for child support rests with parents . . . there is agreement that whether children live with both parents, or just one, able-bodied parents have a responsibility to support their children by working. Toward this end we ought to remove the barriers to employment.
>
> (US Government 1987b: 3)

Senator Moynihan's sentiments were repeated in *Children Come First* which announced:

> The Government proposes to establish a system of child maintenance which will . . . ensure that parents meet the cost of their children's maintenance whenever they can without removing the parents' own incentives to work, and go on working. [And] enable caring parents who wish to work to do so as soon as they feel ready and able.
>
> (DSS 1990: Volume I, p. 5)

In July 1989 the Social Security Advisory Committee (SSAC) continued with this theme in *Why Don't They Go to Work? Mothers on Benefit*. This report found 'evidence that lone mothers who receive regular maintenance at a reasonable level show a markedly increased propensity to work' (Brown 1989: 3).

The change in attitudes towards women in work was closely associated with the desire to reinforce the work ethic discussed in the previous chapter. In both the United States and Britain the social security system was designed with the underlying assumption that women with children would not enter the labour market. In the US this assumption gradually changed as women, even with young children, began to do so. By the time of the passage of the 1988 FSA it was assumed that women with children, even children as young as one year old, should work.

As noted in *Why Don't They Go to Work?*, similar changes were occurring in women's working patterns and in the attitudes towards single mothers in Britain:

> the social security system was planned on the further assumption that it was not in the interest of children for a married woman to go out to work . . . the large scale return to the labour force of married women with dependent children has raised questions about this policy.
>
> (Brown 1989: 1)

Under the Blair government this attitude has continued into the late 1990s, as can be seen with the advent of the 'National Child Care Strategy' and the 'New Deal' for lone parents.

As part of the Thatcher government's neo-liberal philosophy and supply-side economic approach it placed an emphasis on the reduction of the Public Sector Borrowing Requirement (PSBR) at the expense of other social and economic goals. This economic approach to the development of social policy further attracted the government to the American welfare-to-work system and, in particular, its CSES component. Certainly, proponents of the 1988 FSA advocated the inclusion of the child support enforcement requirements in Title I as a means of reducing the government's welfare budget. As was noted in *Congressional Quarterly Weekly Report*:

> Moynihan has made the child-support provisions the first title of his bill, in keeping with a theme . . . that the welfare problem is primarily one of parental responsibility. Another reason for including the provisions, he conceded, is their political appeal . . . Perhaps most significant, though, is the fact that the provisions not only pay for themselves, they raise money to help pay for the rest of the bill.
>
> (Rovner 1988: 1648)

The desire to use the Child Support Agency to reduce the PSBR is similarly apparent in *Children Come First*. The opening pages of Cm 1264 announce that the CSA was designed to ensure that lone parents would: 'avoid . . . becoming dependent on Income Support whenever this is possible and, where it is not possible, to minimise the period of dependence' (DSS 1990: 5). Further evidence of the government's desire to use the Child Support Agency to decrease the PSBR was provided in the Agency's business plan which set the Agency a target of reducing the PSBR by £530 million annually (DSS 1993a).

Historical record

Finally, the Thatcher government was also drawn to the American child support enforcement system because it was perceived as a well-established system which had been highly studied and publicized for over 16 years before the introduction of *Children Come First*. In 1974, in response to growing concern over the lack of co-ordination and consistency in the awarding and size of child support, Congress passed the Social Service Amendments. These established the basis of the American CSES. For the next 14 years Congress continued to adjust the system developed within these Amendments until the passage of the 1988 FSA. As this indicates, the Thatcher government had ample opportunity to study what it perceived as a highly developed system before introducing the British CSA.

While the above section has demonstrated some of the reasons the Thatcher government transferred the American CSES to Britain it has not established that the government was aware of, and interested in, drawing lessons from the American CSES, in particular Wisconsin's CSA. Both of these conditions must be demonstrated before it can be established that policy transfer occurred. Thus in the following section I will demonstrate that the Thatcher government was aware of the American CSES, in particular the Wisconsin CSA. Where appropriate, I will also show where the Thatcher government drew upon the Australian CSA. Finally, in the following section I will demonstrate that the government was interested in adopting lessons from both the United States and Australia.

There was knowledge of, and interest in, the American CSES prior to the development of the CSA

Reportedly, the process of borrowing the American CSES began at a Paris conference in 1986 when David Willetts, a member of the Downing Street Policy Unit, met Irwin Garfinkel, one of the key people studying and advising policy makers on the design and operation of the American CSES. After their meeting it was reported that David Willetts wrote to Prime Minister Thatcher about the American CSES. Upon receiving this report she was allegedly 'rapturous: nail the guilty fathers and at the same time cut hundreds of millions off the Social Security budget – give the man a rise' (Popham 1994: 124)! Four years after the Paris conference the government announced its intention to implement the CSA with the same structure, guidelines and functions as its American counterpart.

More direct evidence of the government's borrowing of the American CSES was provided in *Children Come First* which announced that the 'Secretary of State and senior officials visited the United States to talk to the judiciary and officials involved in the operation of the child support systems there' (DSS 1990: Volume II, p. 85).[16] *Children Come First* continues with a detailed description of the Wisconsin child support system. In particular, *Children Come First* highlights Wisconsin's use of a formula to determine the value of child support awards and the use of wage withholding to ensure absent parents make their payments (pp. 85–6). All these elements were later integrated into the British CSA. In fact, while not fully implemented by either the 1991 or 1995 Acts, the Labour government has recommended in *Children First* that, just as in the US, a system of wage withholding be implemented when direct payment arrangements break down (DSS 1998a: 29).

The Security Advisory Committee's report, *Why Don't They Go to Work?* (Brown 1989), also examined the alterations to the American child support enforcement system made by the 1974 Social Service Amendments; the 1984 Child Support Enforcement Amendments; and the 1988 Family Support Act. Not only does *Why Don't They Go to Work?* examine America's CSES but it also reviews the AFDC programme dating back to its inception as the Aid to Dependent Children (ADC) programme in the 1935 Social Security Act.

Further evidence of the government's interest in, and use of, the American CSES in the development of the CSA was provided by Gillian Shephard. On 12 February 1990 she argued in the House of Commons that:

> We are particularly concerned about the number of lone-parent families on benefit here who receive little or no maintenance. We are therefore examining the whole maintenance system to establish how it can be improved. As part of this process we are examining maintenance arrangements abroad, including those in the United States, to see whether there are any lessons to be learned from them.
>
> (Hansard 1990)

The above section provides ample evidence that the government was aware of, and interested in, the American CSES. Conclusive evidence of the government's reliance on the American, and more specifically the Wisconsin, model was presented by a high-ranking official at the Department of Social Security (DSS) who recounted that not only was the Department studying the Wisconsin model but that it was 'very clearly used in the development of the Child Support Agency'.[17]

What was transferred from the American CSES?

This section is divided into four parts. The first part will provide a overview of how the British child support enforcement system operated prior to the establishment of the Child Support Agency. The second part provides a review of the Australian influence on the development of the Agency. The third part examines how the American child support enforcement system emerged and operated, at the federal level, from 1974 through to the passage of the 1988 Family Support Act. The final part provides a review of the key elements of the British Child Support Agency borrowed from America.

Britain before 1993

Before 1993 Britain had a system of awarding and collecting child support through the Department of Social Security (DSS) and the court system. This system was characterized by adversarial negotiations; wide variations in child support awards, due to the discretionary nature of the system; the absence of a systematic procedure to ensure benefits were uprated in line with inflation, the changing circumstances of the parent ordered to provide child support, or the custodial parent; and the near universal failure of the absent parent to make full child support payments. Consequently, it was argued that the court-based system

> resulted in differences in the maintenance received by lone parent families which bore little relationship to their needs or to the circumstance of

former partners . . . Additionally the living standards of 'second' families tended to be protected in maintenance assessments, whereas the majority of 'first' families – lone mothers and their children – lived on means-tested benefits.

(Craig *et al.* 1996: 108)

The CSA was established in response to the perceived 'failure' of the existing system; the government's neo-liberal outlook; and the government's desire to reduce the PSBR. The government established the Child Support Agency to eliminate the role of the courts and the DSS in the determination and collection of child support awards. In doing this they made the agency responsible for assessing and collecting child support; creating and implementing a universal formula for calculating an individual's child support maintenance liability; and forcing all parents claiming state benefits to cooperate in the recovery of child support maintenance through the identification of the liable parent, unless they could prove that doing so would place them and their children at risk. All of these provisions were borrowed by the Thatcher government from the American child support enforcement systems.

Australia

While the American child support enforcement system, and in particular the Wisconsin CSAS, was the primary model used to develop the CSA, it should be noted that the Australian Child Support Agency (itself based upon the American CSES) was also influential in the development of the CSA. As noted in *Children Come First*:

as part of the survey of the maintenance system in Great Britain the DSS carried out a literature study to look at the way other countries enforce child support provisions. The maintenance systems studied included . . . New Zealand, Australia and . . . the USA . . . [In addition] senior officers attending a social security conference in Australia in November 1989 were also able to learn first hand about the new Australian Child Support Agency.

(DSS 1990: Volume II, p. 85)

Children Come First also stresses that 'Australia had many of the same concerns as Great Britain about the adequacy of their maintenance system and conducted in depth research before choosing the present radical system' (DSS 1990: Volume II, p. 85). In addition to discussing the American CSES, *Why Don't They Go to Work?* (Brown 1989) also examines the Australian child support enforcement system and Agency, actually calling attention to its use of the American CSES in the development of the Australian system. Thus, Australia's CSES was important not only as a model but because it demonstrated to the Thatcher government that the American child support enforcement system, particularly the Wisconsin model, could be successfully transferred and used in a foreign environment to address problems similar to those British policy makers perceived themselves as facing.

The American system

To help understand the key elements integrated into the British CSA borrowed from America it is useful to begin with a brief discussion of how the American system operated between 1974 and 1988. In the United States, concern over the operation and application of the child support system and the way the courts determined maintenance awards reached the political agenda by the early 1970s. This concern compelled Congress to pass the 1974 Social Service Amendments. These Amendments required every state to establish a child support enforcement system.[18] As part of this, states had to establish 'special agencies for the collection of child support payments due to recipients of AFDC who were required to sign over to the state claims to child support as a condition of [AFDC] eligibility' (Archibald 1986: 203). Moreover, state child support enforcement agencies were given the authority and responsibility for 'locating absent parents, establishing paternity, preparing support orders, monitoring compliance with support orders, distributing collections, and periodically reviewing and modifying support orders' (Adams *et al.* 1992: 668). The 1974 Amendments also required states to establish parent locator services 'that could request information from the Social Security Administration and the Internal Revenue Service', on the location and income of absentee parents. Finally, states were required to 'offer similar services to non–AFDC cases if requested' (Archibald 1986: 203).

Widespread dissatisfaction with the implementation and results of the 1974 Act, particularly within the Reagan administration, forced Congress to amend the Act with the passage of the 1984 Child Support Enforcement Amendments. Specifically, Section 3 of the 1984 Child Support Enforcement Amendments required every state's child support enforcement agency to establish procedures for automatically withholding income from the pay and tax refunds of absentee parents, whenever their child support payments fell into arrears of over one month, without having to request court intervention.[19] Section 3 also required states to establish procedures imposing 'lines against real and personal property for the amount of overdue support . . . [and] permitted states to extend withholding to income other than wages, such as bonuses and commissions, or dividends' (Congressional Quarterly 1985: 606). Sections 15 and 18 required states to establish a committee responsible for formulating child support award guidelines based upon a standardized formula. Once established, these guidelines were to be provided to 'all judges and other officials who have the power to determine child support awards within such state, but need not be binding' (US Government 1984: Section 15).

Title I of the 1988 FSA continued the development of the American child support enforcement system. Section 101 of Title I requires every state to implement various procedures for immediate and mandatory wage withholding for all support orders being enforced by the state's CSEA. The only exception to this is if either a judge rules there is a 'good cause' for not enforcing the rules or if both parents sign an agreement specifying other arrangements. Section 101 also requires the Agency to begin such procedures upon the request of either parent or the Agency. Section 102 strengthens the 1984 requirement that the first $50 collected in support payments does not count as income for benefit entitlement purposes. Section 103 mandated that the child support award guidelines established by the 1984 Child Support Enforcement Amendments 'must be applied by judges and other officials in determining the amount of any child support award unless the judge or official . . . makes a finding that there is good cause for not applying the guidelines' (US Government 1988: Section 103). Section 103 also required states to 'periodically review and adjust' all child support orders being enforced by the Agency. Finally, Section 111 strengthens and extends state obligations to establish the paternity of every child in relation to AFDC cases. This was included in the Act so that the Agency could establish and enforce child support obligations whenever an absent parent denied that they were the father or mother of the child, or children, in question. The only exceptions to this rule were for 'a child who is receiving cash benefits by reason of the death of a parent, or a child with respect to whom a mother is found to have good cause for refusing to co-operate in establishing or collecting support' (US Government 1988: Section 111).

As will be demonstrated below, each element of the American child support enforcement system outlined above was transferred into the design of the British Child Support Agency.

The British system

In *Children Come First* the government specified the functions of the Child Support Agency:

> to identify and trace liable persons if their whereabouts are unknown; to obtain information on the incomes and circumstance of the parents of the child for whom maintenance is claimed . . . to assess the maintenance to be paid . . . to record and monitor the payments made where appropriate; to take appropriate enforcement action at an early date when payments are not made; to review the assessment at regular intervals.
>
> (DSS 1990: Volume I, p. 31)

The above quote reveals the basic similarities between the American child support enforcement system and the British Child Support Agency. However, it is worth examining some of the CSA's operational guidelines to illustrate the similarities.

The 1988 FSA required states to determine child support orders based on the formula developed in response to the Child Support Enforcement Amendments of 1984. Based upon American experience, and in particular the formula structure developed in Wisconsin, the Thatcher government required the CSA to establish maintenance obligations based upon a formula. As described in *Children Come First*, the formula would be an 'assessment of how much maintenance should be paid . . . [and] will apply to all families where maintenance is an issue and therefore eliminate any scope for inconsistency' (DSS 1990: Volume I, p. 6).

As in the United States, state CSES are also under legal obligation to undertake regular reviews of child support awards to ensure they are kept in line with the changing circumstances of the parents and the rate of inflation. As noted in *Children Come First*:

> The Government proposes to establish a system of child maintenance which will be equally available to any person seeking maintenance . . . and which will . . . allow for maintenance payments to be reviewed regularly so that changes in circumstances can be taken into account automatically [without recourse to the courts].
>
> (DSS 1990: Volume I, p. 5)

There are also provisions in both the United States and Britain to ensure, when administrators assessed and reviewed child support awards, that second families were not damaged by the amount of the award granted and that an absent parent had a basic minimum income protected within the formula. Specifically, Cm 1264 states that the CSA must

> recognise that where a liable parent has formed a second family and has further natural children, he is liable to maintain all his own children. A fair and reasonable balance has to be struck between the interests of the children of a first family and the children of a second.
>
> (DSS 1990: Volume I, p. 5)

This was expressed within the regulations governing 'exempt income' which was to be maintained at the 'protected level'. In the United States this level was set at 55 per cent of disposable income for fathers with a second family and 65 per cent for those living alone.[20]

One of the mechanisms available to the CSA to ensure payment of income support is automatic income withholding. While the ability of the CSA to choose whether to impose automatic income withholding may seem to be a significant difference between the United States and Britain, this was not a true 'requirement' within the American CSES. While the 1984 Amendments required state Agencies automatically to withhold earnings from parents who fell into arrears of one month or over, and the 1988 FSA mandated that all cases handled by a state's Agency use automatic withholding of support awards, both Acts allowed parents to agree to other arrangements. Due to these provisions the majority of parents developed alternative arrangements for the payment of child support awards. In fact, by 1990 only 44 per cent of all child support cases were using automatic income withholding for the enforcement of child support payments. The flexibility that was implicitly built into the American CSES was thus explicitly expressed in the rules governing the British CSA.

In the United States AFDC (now TANF) recipients are required to help the child support enforcement agency determine the paternity of their children. They are also required to claim child support, unless they have a 'good cause' for refusing to cooperate. If an individual is found not to have a good cause, he or she, but not any of their children, faces losing his or her benefit entitlement.

Given the government's concerns for finding ways to reduce the PSBR, it should come as no surprise that these provisions were transferred directly into the provisions governing the CSA:

> When the caring parent is receiving Income Support or Family Credit, the taxpayer has an interest in whether maintenance is paid. In these circumstances, the parent will be required to make a claim for maintenance to the Agency . . . There will be exceptions where this is not in the interest of the children. Where there is no such good cause for declining to seek maintenance, the allowance for the caring parent, but not that for the children, may be reduced.
>
> (DSS 1990: Volume I, p. ii)

The government's desire to use the Agency as a mechanism for the reduction of the PSBR led it to design the Agency's regulations to reduce benefits for up to 18 months for any parent refusing to cooperate in the identification of the liable parent unless they could prove they had a 'good cause' for not helping in this process.

Both the 1984 Child Support Enforcement Amendments and the 1988 FSA required states to transfer the first $50 of any child support collected to the family. Moreover, the $50 was to be disregarded for the purposes of determining welfare eligibility. Though not as generous as American regulations, due to the government's desire to use the Agency to reduce the PSBR, this was replicated in the rules governing the CSA. Specifically, the Act guarantees that 'Caring parents who receive Family Credit, Housing Benefit or Community Charge Benefit will not have the first £15 of maintenance received taken into account in calculating their income' (DSS 1990: Volume I, p. iii).[21]

The 1974 Social Services Amendments, together with the 1984 Child Support Enforcement Amendments and the 1988 Family Support Act, required all non-AFDC families seeking the services of the child support enforcement agency to be charged a minimal fee for its services. As a result of the government's desire to use the Agency as a cost-saving device this philosophy was also transferred to the CSA. Specifically, the Agency was established so that it was required to charge all clients not receiving income support 'for the assessment and collection of maintenance', even when they are required to use the Agency in the assessment and collection of child support (DSS 1993b: 6).

Finally, as part of the child support enforcement system, federal and state governments were required to operate parent locator services capable of accessing information from state agencies, the Department of Health and Human Services, the Internal Revenue Services and the Department of Labor. The

Service was designed to provide information on the location of absent parents, their place of employment and their income, at the request of the child support enforcement agency. This service was transferred into the structure of the CSA:

> In some cases, the present whereabouts are unknown and, in still fewer cases, the identity is not known for certain. The Department of Social Security already has powers to use its own records of names and addresses and the Inland Revenue's records of names and addresses of individuals and their employers to help locate liable persons . . . The Child Support Agency will need similar powers.
>
> (DSS 1993b: 32)[22]

How did the policy transfer process lead to implementation 'failure'?

Although the Thatcher government transferred the design and structure of the Child Support Agency from the United States, it soon became apparent that the Agency was not operating as the government had originally hoped. Moreover, as *Children First* testifies, despite numerous functional and administrative changes the Agency continues to be perceived as a failure among both policy makers and many of the families subjected to the Agency's intervention. This section will demonstrate that these problems partially resulted from inappropriate policy transfer. In particular, three factors had a significant impact on the Agency's effectiveness: first, it is clear that the Thatcher government had insufficient information about how the American CSES operated; second, although transfer occurred, crucial elements of what made the American and Australian systems 'successful' were not transferred; third, insufficient attention was paid to the differences between the social, political and ideological contexts in which the American CSES operated. More specifically, the government had insufficient understanding of how the American system worked and consequently failed to recognize how the American CSES relied upon other system variables for its 'success', particularly the continuing importance of the courts in the operation of the US CSES; and as has already been mentioned, it regarded the CSA primarily as a means of controlling the Public Sector Borrowing Requirement (PSBR).

Although the British government consciously set out to draw lessons from the United States they concentrated on the Wisconsin system. The key point is that there should have been a more thorough analysis of how the CSES system worked in other US states, particularly the formula (for Wisconsin operated what was in some ways the most regressive of three basic types), and indeed of the Australian CSA, which itself drew lessons from the US experience. Had this taken place, it is likely that the government would have discovered some of the drawbacks of the Wisconsin system (and its formula), and how important the courts remained in the operation of the CSES in most US states.

As important as the lack of knowledge was in subsequent problems experienced by the CSA, a second factor might have had an even greater impact upon its failure: the British government imposed the CSA into and over the pre-existing system governing the granting and collection of child support maintenance. In particular, the legislation which established the CSA set aside prior court and DSS maintenance arrangements. This was bound to cause dissatisfaction, especially among couples who had agreed their existing agreements. More importantly, the Agency replaced the courts and the DSS, although this was not the case in either the United States or Australia. In fact, the government failed to realize how important the courts and the DSS were in acting as an escape valve for both the Agency and the individuals involved. For example, the initial legislation established the Agency so that it had no discretion in the amount of child support an absent parent was required to pay. Because of this, and the fact that the courts were no longer part of the maintenance assessment or collection process, individual circumstances could no longer be taken into consideration. Moreover, the formula had to be used even when couples had come to an equitable agreement within the court system. This problem was compounded by the fact that, initially, the British formula, unlike that in most American states or Australia, neglected to take into account any property or capital settlements which the couple had agreed.

Overall, by failing to learn lessons from the US, the government reduced the ability of individuals to comply with the settlements being imposed upon them by the CSA, and increased the likelihood that all parties would be dissatisfied with the results of CSA decisions. In fact, dissatisfaction with the results of CSA decisions was so extensive that, even among mothers receiving help from the Agency, there was 'outrage at the levels of maintenance now being demanded from former partners, which they felt were unrelated to either their children's actual needs or to the actual weekly benefit levels to which they were expected to feed and clothe their children' (Craig et al. 1996: 113). One mother was even quoted as saying: 'They've got to stop asking for so much . . . they're asking for sums beyond belief' (Clarke et al. 1994: 109). This situation has continued and has probably become worse since the 1995 Act. As stressed on the first page of *Children First*: 'Over 70 per cent of lone mothers on Income Support seek to avoid making a child support application. Most parents do not trust the child support scheme to treat them fairly.' The report continues: 'A scheme which never gained the consent of non-resident parents has now lost support amongst the majority of parents with care' (DSS 1998a: 1, 12).

Equally important, in both the United States and Australia the revised child support enforcement systems were phased in so that any problems, particularly those involving discrepancies between the old and new systems, could be reduced by making any necessary changes. If the British government had learned this lesson, instead of simply imposing the CSA immediately onto a pre-existing system, the likelihood is that the CSA would have experienced fewer implementation problems, for as problems arose they could have been corrected before widespread public and political outrage formed.

In developing the Child Support Agency the Thatcher government made the Agency's prime objective the reduction in benefit expenditure on lone parents. This was part of the government's overall strategy, inspired by their commitment to neo-liberalism, to reduce the PSBR by attacking government spending, particularly in relation to welfare programmes. Indeed, this emphasis was clear from the earliest days of the Conservatives' interest in US experience. This emphasis on the primacy of cutting government expenditure greatly affected the way in which the CSA operated. In addition, as Craig, Glendinning and Clarke observe: 'in making one objective – the reduction in welfare benefit expenditure on lone parents – paramount . . . The government failed to . . . learn the lessons of relevant experiences from within the UK and elsewhere' (1996: 107).

Indeed, the strategy led to serious implementation problems. For example, by using the Agency to reduce the PSBR the government altered the target group most affected by the Agency. In the US and Australia the prime groups targeted were individuals who had fallen into arrears or who were not making any child support payments. In Britain, the primary target group became those who could make the biggest contribution to reducing the PSBR. As noted in a leaked Agency document: 'This is not the time for the cases we know should get early attention . . . The name of the game is maximising the maintenance yield – don't waste a lot of time on non-profitable stuff!'(cited in Graham and Knights 1994: 70). By going after 'soft' targets, instead of non-payers, the Agency reduced its legitimacy in the eyes of the public and also drifted away from one of the basic characteristics of the American CSES. In the United States and Australia the child support enforcement systems were not designed 'primarily' to reduce the PSBR. Rather, the US and Australia developed their child support enforcement systems to redress the problems inherent in federal systems dominated by the judiciary in the award of child support payments. Most importantly, when the United States and Australia were developing their systems, officials continually stressed that the major reason for developing the CSES was to address the growing problem of single parents becoming dependent upon state aid; not to reduce government expenditure. In fact, in the United States the CSES was grounded in policies designed to get single mothers back into the workforce. This was most clearly reflected in the 1988 Family Support Act which developed a system of work, education, training, child care and other support services in order to help single mothers in receipt of AFDC benefits to re-enter the regular job market. This meant it was easier to generate support for the policy than in Britain where it was widely seen as illegitimate to attack parents who were already paying considerable maintenance.

Overall, by changing the primary goal of the Agency and focusing on reducing the PSBR, the Thatcher government failed to understand how the CSA's other objectives would be compromised, leading to significant implementation problems.

Agency revisions

While the British Child Support Agency had its origins in the American child support enforcement system, many of the safety mechanisms and underlying purposes built into the American system were either not transferred or were muted in their incorporation into the British system. As a result, complaints began mounting over the operation of the CSA. By 1994 the appearance of failure became so extensive that the government was forced to introduce a number of changes to the Agency. For example, in December 1993 the government passed an Amendment requiring the Agency to recalculate all completed assessments. In December 1994, the Secretary of State announced that the originally planned extension of the Agency's remit to include parents who had been contacted before July 1994 but had not responded, and lone parents in receipt of means-tested benefits before the Act came into effect, but who had not been contacted, was to be 'shelved indefinitely'. These changes continued into 1995 when the government was forced to reduce the savings targets of the Agency, and adjust the formula to include a 'departure system' which allows the Agency some discretion in the allocation of the formula. This alteration in the functioning of the formula is extremely important because it was one of the primary features always present in the American system but not incorporated into the Agency. At this time the government announced that lone parents not in receipt of means-tested benefits and who had already agreed to court-arranged maintenance agreements were not, as originally planned, to be dealt with by the Agency. *Children First* proposes further changes to the CSA. Some of the more dramatic of these are a further change in the design and operation of the formula; special provisions for absent parents whose net income is between £100 and £200 per week; the introduction of wage withholding; the introduction of a £10 maintenance premium; and, unlike the Thatcher or Major governments, *Children First* proposes implementing these changes in three stages so that alterations can be made as necessary.

These changes have brought the British CSA closer to the design and operation of the American CSES. However, it remains to be seen if they will overcome the implementation problems created by the incomplete, and in some ways inappropriate, transfer of the American system. This possibility is looking increasingly likely as the Blair government continues to emphasize the Agency's role in reducing the welfare state bill directed toward single parents and their children.

Conclusion

While most scholars examining the Child Support Agency discuss its performance, this chapter has focused upon the development of the British Child Support Agency and how this development helps explain why the Agency has experienced systematic implementation problems. Utilizing a policy transfer framework helps explain both why and how the government developed the Agency and why the CSA did not work as the government originally hoped.

In order to establish both of these points, this chapter was divided into four sections. First, it examined why the government decided to develop the Agency, rather than continuing with the court-based child support award system. The government turned mainly to the American experience because similar changes were occurring in the structure of the labour market and the wider society in the United States and Britain: more women were entering the labour market; there was a dramatic rise in the number of single parent families, with the majority of these families depending on state benefits for their survival; the number of women receiving child support awards and the amount of those awards showed considerable variation, even in cases with similar circumstances; and a large number of women were not receiving child support, even when awarded. Second, it was demonstrated how parallel developments in Britain and the United States led the Thatcher government first to be interested in, and then to borrow the key elements of, the American CSES. Third, this chapter highlighted the extent to which the key elements of the Child Support Agency were directly transferred from the United States. Finally, it was shown that inappropriate policy transfer offers an important, even if partial, explanation of the CSA's implementation problems and why two successive governments have spent considerable legislative time attempting to correct the mistakes initially integrated into the CSA.

3

Health: the 'internal market' and reform of the National Health Service

Fiona O'Neill

Health care has always been an area which has lent itself to a wider dissemination of ideas and policies than the purely national. A spirit of cooperation, reinforced by a medical ethic which naturally predisposes towards sharing resources and expertise, has found expression and reinforcement through international organizations like the Red Cross and the World Health Organization (WHO), as well as within the less formal networking and exchange of ideas, which continues to influence and inform practitioners and policy makers alike. Since the 1980s the diffusion and exchange of ideas at the international level has reached a new intensity as the perspectives of policy makers from Australia to Sweden have become increasingly defined by anxieties about how demographic changes, technological advances and rising public expectations could affect future health care expenditure. The search for cost-effective solutions to the challenge represented by escalating health costs helped fuel a growing interest in comparative health care and a desire to understand how different health care systems were organized, financed and delivered. Extensive programmes of reform were started in many Western developed countries and a number of common themes can be found within the reform strategies pursued by governments administering quite different health care systems (OECD 1992, 1994). This period of rapid change and transformation contains rich material for the application of the policy transfer model as globe-trotting policy makers, academics and health care practitioners participated in what has become an increasingly transnational debate about health care reform.

The background to reform

This chapter will focus on the considerable changes which have taken place in the British National Health Service (NHS) and examine how far reforms implemented by the British governments of the late 1980s and early 1990s were informed by ideas and policy prescriptions generated in America. Some commentators have argued that there has been an 'Americanization' of the NHS following the adoption of market-oriented health policies which were exported across the Atlantic (Health Policy Network 1996). Certainly, the introduction of the 'internal market' which was the central plank of the reforms introduced in the White Paper *Working for Patients* (WFP) (DoH 1989), and implemented by the Thatcher government in 1991, drew heavily on the ideas of the American health economist Alain Enthoven. Robin Cook, speaking at the time as the Labour Party front-bench spokesman on health, summed up the fears of many when he proclaimed that the orientation of the WFP proposals would inexorably lead to 'market medicine as it is practised across the Atlantic' (Klein 1995: 192). While recent policy initiatives in the NHS have moved away from an emphasis on markets and competition, American influence is still highly relevant and the chapter will include a brief outline of how 'managed care', which has assumed a central role within American health policy, is now attracting a lot of attention in Britain.

Careful analysis needs to be undertaken before too many assumptions are made about the influence of America on the development of the NHS. Health care has become a highly politicized area of public policy. Ideological battles rage about every aspect of health policy, and the market reforms created an unprecedented outpouring of hostility from health professionals, opposition groups and the official Opposition alike. Comparisons with America have been handy ammunition for use by those seeking to highlight deficiencies in the new NHS. In reality, the changes to the NHS have been driven by a number of factors including underlying social, economic and technological trends, which are transforming the delivery of health care in all advanced industrial countries. Formal policy change, as initiated by government, needs to be put into this wider context. Explanations of change which place a disproportionate emphasis on any one factor, including policy transfer, are in danger of giving the reform process a coherence and neatness that it probably lacked. The reality of health care reform is a messy and disparate process, in which any one variable, such as policy transfer, is just one among many competing influences which have shaped the overall process of reform.

Things are not always as they seem

The events described in this chapter demonstrate that policy transfer did not act as an independent variable, capable of explaining why the Thatcher government introduced the internal market reforms into the NHS. While American ideas about health care reform influenced the content of British reforms, and these imported ideas did have certain implications, particularly in terms of the severe implementation problems that followed their introduction, these ideas were not inherently attractive for their own sake. The Thatcher and Major governments, in common with their counterparts in other Western industrialized nations, were actively seeking ways of containing the share of the budget directed at health care, while at the same time attempting to adapt to the climate of change within the NHS. This climate was created by factors such as the rapid developments in medical technology which were beginning to affect the nature of the British health care system profoundly. At the same time ideas about health reform, associated with American health economists, assumed something of an international currency, being well known and rehearsed within international policy-making circles since the early 1980s. These ideas appealed to the Thatcher and Major governments for a variety of reasons, though most were connected with domestic circumstances rather than arising from a strong motivation to emulate American experience.

In fact, the 'internal market' was from the start an abstraction that had no concrete existence in the American, or indeed, any other health care system. While the idea of competition and other market-type innovations, which the WFP reforms incorporated, can be clearly aligned with developments in health care across the Atlantic, and were actively promoted by American health economists such ideas did not represent a ready-made blueprint for reforming the NHS, capable of wholesale importation.

The role of policy transfer in this case was to act as a catalyst which helped to focus the minds of those involved in the reform process on a particular set of solutions. But the reasons why those solutions appeared attractive and the precise way that imported ideas were combined with 'home-grown' innovations is largely due to factors internal to the British system. Specifically, the perception of a mounting 'crisis' in the NHS demanded some response. However, while the nature of the 'crisis' was ostensibly financial, the government had to focus on options that would transform the service without being unduly burdensome on the public purse (given its desire to reduce the PSBR). More importantly, the government had to find a way to transform the NHS which did not challenge its founding principles in a politically explosive way. As policy makers looked around for solutions to this dilemma the high profile that American market-centred theories of health care had assumed within policy-making circles provided an accessible and acceptable source of ideas to build upon. Moreover, these ideas were appealing to policy makers because they could work while retaining the founding principles; promised to improve the cost-efficiency of the service, without demanding extra resources; built on the managerial reforms which had started in 1983; were in tune with the reform enacted in other public sector services, such as education; and they appealed to the ideological foundations of the Thatcher government. However, there was little in the way of hard evidence to substantiate the theoretical claims of Enthoven and his associates, and in many ways the implementation of the internal market was a leap in the dark.

These points illustrate that the origins of the *Working for Patients* reforms, in common with most other pieces of public policy, are complex and not amenable to reduction down to a single explanatory variable. But while policy transfer cannot, and should not, claim to be able to explain all or even most aspects of the internal market reforms, the utility of the model is in highlighting those areas in which policy transfer, from America, did play a part in shaping the overall direction that the reform took. An opportunity then arises to examine certain details of the reform strategy in more depth and raise a number of questions about the nature and effect of the reforms. In particular a case can be made that the transfer of American ideas about health care was particularly inappropriate for the British health care system. This inappropriateness can at least partially explain the severe implementation problems that followed the implementation of the *Working for Patients* policies. The market-oriented aspects of the reforms most closely associated with the American health care system became the major focus for dissent and symbolized for many the threat to a long-cherished public institution. Such hostility contributed to the highly charged political atmosphere which characterized the health policy arena in the 1980s and early 1990s. Margaret Thatcher's declaration at the 1982 Tory Party Conference that the NHS is 'safe in our hands' had a particularly hollow ring for many caught up in the maelstrom created by the reforms.

Change is all around

The case of the internal market by no means exhausts the areas of change in health policy which were effected by policy transfer from America. Other areas such as the expansion of the paramedic service, the growth in day surgery, and a growing interest in topics such as informed consent, living wills and physician-assisted suicide, all have detectable roots in America but are less clearly identifiable as part of the main reform strategy. Likewise there have been important changes in working practices among health care professionals which have unfolded independently of the reform process, but which also have roots in American practice. This is particularly true of changes in the way that nursing care is organized and delivered which has fundamentally altered the nursing care that patients receive and which was heavily influenced by American literature and experience (Beardshaw 1992). In addition, the activities of American health corporations involved in the delivery of for-profit private health care is rapidly becoming another source of American influence as saturated markets in America drive companies to look for new opportunities elsewhere (Smith 1997).

The 'Working for Patients' review

The NHS dominated the 1987 general election campaign and, as Mrs Thatcher's third term of office got under way, stories of ward closures, lengthening waiting lists and postponed operations continued to capture the headlines. The mood of crisis was strengthened by vocal professional discontent as the Presidents of the Royal Colleges publicly denounced the government's policies, issuing an appeal 'to save our National Health Service, once the envy of the world' (Timmins 1995: 24). The highly charged atmosphere was compounded by a commonly held belief by policy makers and analysts alike that the Griffiths reforms implemented in 1983 had only a partial effect and that the principles behind the reform had yet to reach their logical conclusion. Briefly, the Griffiths reforms replaced the previous system of administration with a new system of general management heavily influenced by private sector management styles (Saltman and von Otter 1992).

Thus, a review of the NHS had become inevitable. It was against this background of financial crisis, professional discontent and an ever-embarrassing political situation, that Mrs Thatcher announced the formation of an official review of the NHS. It was this review which lead to the publication of *Working for Patients*, in January 1989.

The way the review was conducted reflected the rejection of the consensual style of politics which had previously characterized the health policy process. A small Cabinet Committee chaired by the Prime Minister conducted the review. Specialist advisers were invited to give evidence but there was no attempt to mount the kind of consultative process that had marked previous NHS reviews. Those NHS doctors and managers who were invited to meetings were known for their support of more radical ideas. While the review had been ostensibly precipitated by a financial crisis, it left the system of funding the NHS unchanged. Klein argues that the review was characterized by 'reluctant radicalism' (1995: 183). Despite mounting speculation that the Thatcher administration intended, in essence, to abolish the existing NHS by, for example, moving to an insurance-based system, WFP left the founding principles of the NHS intact. The government reaffirmed its commitment to a health service funded out of general taxation and delivering comprehensive health care to the entire population. Once the government had ruled out major structural change, the review team were left with options which would change the delivery rather than the financial basis of the service. In this way, the *Working for Patients* proposals can be seen as an attempt to change the dynamics of the system while leaving the basic principles of the NHS intact. It was this interest in the delivery of services that led the review team to draw on American ideas about the application of market principles to health care reform in general and the idea of an 'internal market' as suggested by Alain Enthoven specifically.

Reflections of an American health economist: the internal market

Professor Alain Enthoven had been an Assistant US Secretary of State for Defense in the Johnson era and was acknowledged to be one of America's leading experts on the economics and management of health services. In 1984 he spent several weeks studying the management of the NHS. His initial visit was sponsored by the Nuffield Provincial Hospitals who invited Enthoven to take a 'sympathetic' look at the NHS. The Nuffield Provincial Hospital Trust then published *Reflections on the Management of the National Health Service*, containing Enthoven's analysis and conclusions. *Reflections on the Management of the National Health Service* (Enthoven 1985) identifies a number of problems with the management and organizational structure of the NHS which, in sum, are alleged to have trapped the NHS in a 'gridlock', making real change very difficult to achieve. A number of problem areas are identified as contributing to a system characterized by inertia. These include the intense politicization of the NHS, making politicians cautious and generating a more generalized aversion to trying anything new; a private sector 'escape valve' which removes the voice of more articulate sections of the population; a system of incentives which does little to reward efficiency-improving changes; the power and autonomy vested in hospital consultants and general practitioners (GPs) due to existing contractual arrangements; and the nationally negotiated agreements with nurses and other unionized staff which makes changes to working practices difficult to impose.

While expressing some sympathy with the objectives of the Griffiths management reforms, Enthoven was pessimistic that they could achieve anything more than cosmetic change. Part of the problem, he argued, was the desire to maintain national uniformity. Perhaps more importantly, he believed that the rapid timescale for achieving the reform prescribed by central government was unrealistic. More fundamentally, Enthoven argued that little could change in the absence of incentives for staff to provide better services. It is here that 'there is a need for "market forces" or some motivating factor that serves the same purpose' (Enthoven 1985: 21).

Enthoven's main proposal was for an 'internal market model' in which each District Health Authority (DHA) would function as a separate nationalized company free to buy and sell services from, and to, other Districts and trade goods and services with the private sector. Such a scheme, Enthoven argued, would free District Managers to use their resources more efficiently by choosing to buy services from producers who provide the best value for money. Pay and working conditions would preferably be negotiated at a local level and other market-type innovations, such as the ability to keep the proceeds from the sales of capital assets, would also be allowed. The model would make cost sensitivity a dominant feature of the NHS, forcing cost-efficiency to the top of the priority list. Enthoven viewed the internal market model as providing the most feasible model for the NHS but identified a major weakness in that it would still lack adequate incentives for decisions to be based on the best interests of patients rather than health service personnel. To address this problem, in an appendix to the report Enthoven outlined an alternative system of organization and finance to be operated through competing Health Maintenance Organizations (HMOs). Since their inception HMOs had become increasingly significant in America, theoretically providing real consumer choice, by making consumers the drivers of change in place of managers acting on consumers' behalf.

Ideas take root

Enthoven's ideas were well known by the time the review took place. Gordon McLachlan, director of the Nuffield Trust, had made sure the report was circulated to all the top people operating within the NHS. Enthoven himself talked directly to a number of people involved in the health policy arena. For example, prior to the publication of the report, John Redwood and David Willetts, of the Downing Street Policy Unit, met Enthoven to discuss the proposed internal market reforms (Timmins 1995: 458). More importantly, Prime Minister Thatcher personally explored Enthoven's ideas with David Willetts and Norman Fowler, the Secretary of State for the Department of Health and Social Security (DHSS). In fact, in her Downing Street Memoirs Mrs Thatcher discusses her interest in Enthoven's ideas. Specifically, in her description of the 'theoretical debates' that took place before the review began she discusses her interest in his ideas concerning the economics of health care and the internal market (Thatcher 1993: 607). Kenneth Clarke, who replaced John Moore as Secretary of State for Health during the review, acknowledged the contribution of Enthoven's ideas supporting the concept of an internal market: 'because it tried to inject into a state-owned system some of the qualities of competition, choice, and measurement of quality that you get in a well-run, private enterprise' (quoted in Ham 1994: 6).

The reflections also attracted interest from the media. The *Economist* reported on Enthoven's 'full, sympathetic and remarkable report' and noted that it 'could be very important' in the reform of the NHS (*Economist*, 22 June 1985: 19–22). An editorial in the *British Medical Journal* (BMJ) gave a more cautious welcome to Enthoven's message, suggesting that the proposals could, if properly piloted and evaluated first, promote better management and improve services to patients. The BMJ's editorial concluded that 'it would be a tragedy if his ideas were not taken seriously' (12 October 1985: 993). In fact, even before the government released *Working for Patients*, some hospitals started to put Enthoven's ideas into practice, in a limited way. For example, some hospitals started to charge other districts for treating their patients. While charges were only on a small scale and mainly for highly specialist services, the idea of an internal market was beginning to take root. 'We are just nibbling away at an internal market at the moment' the doctor in charge of Barts Hospital was quoted as saying in April 1987, 'but I believe it has got to come' (Timmins 1995: 459).

Other influential actors

It was not only Enthoven who was active in promoting market solutions for the NHS. Think tanks such as the Centre for Policy Studies (CPS) and the Health Unit of the Institute of Economic Affairs (IEA) also lent support to the idea of market-oriented policies. David Willetts, who worked in the Downing Street Policy Unit and later as head of the CPS, was well acquainted with the health economists' arguments. The IEA drew directly on the expertise of American health economists, such as Enthoven and Clark Havighurst, to explore the issue of competition in the NHS. In fact, the foreword to one such paper raised the question 'What can we learn from America about the measures necessary to put competition to work in the service of consumers?' (Havighurst *et al.* 1989: Foreword). British health economists, such as Alan Maynard from York University, also became visible in health policy debates during the 1980s. By the time the review team got to work there was a substantial body of ideas advocating the use of American-style market solutions and, while Enthoven's proposals became the focus of the reform, his ideas were very much in tune with the more general ascendancy of the theories and policy prescriptions associated with health economics in the 1980s.

Ideas into action

The influence of ideas on the content of policy depends on their ability not only to reach key policy makers but also to persuade them. The ideas put forward by the health economists and developed and publicized by the various neo-liberal think tanks fell on fertile soil within the Thatcher government and were very much in tune with developments in the other areas of public policy discussed within this book. In this way, the reform of the NHS can be seen as part of the Thatcherite agenda committed to reducing state interference, public expenditure and the public sector borrowing requirement (PSBR), and ideologically in favour of the use of market forces in order to reinvigorate the economy and free the public sector from the monopoly power of providers.

The internal market was at the heart of the *Working for Patients* reforms. Although some of the details of how the market would operate differed from what Enthoven envisaged, the main guiding principles of his market model were embraced wholeheartedly. The purchaser/provider split was the central pivot on which the market would operate. Two sets of purchasing arrangements were proposed. District Health Authorities (DHAs) would be the main purchasers responsible for buying services for their local population. While drawing from Enthoven's recommendations, in a home-grown innovation (apparently thought up by Kenneth Clarke, the new Secretary of State for Health, as he sat on a headland on holiday in Galicia; Timmins 1995: 464), GPs would also be able to choose to take on a purchasing function by becoming GP fundholders, able to use their budgets to buy some hospital services for their patients as well as pay for the drugs they prescribed. Providers would be NHS hospitals who were to be allowed to free themselves from direct health authority management by becoming self-governing trusts and in the most extreme cases private sector organizations. Hospital budgets would no longer be fixed but based on the key principle of money following the patient. This meant that provider units would, in principle, have to compete for the patients and resources and so have the incentive which Enthoven thought so necessary to improve their performance in terms of efficiency, cost-effectiveness and quality. The system was to operate through the use of contracts and service agreements to provide the links between purchasers and providers. The *Working for Patients* proposals were incorporated into the NHS and Community Care Bill which received Royal Assent in June 1990, and the NHS internal market came into operation in April 1991. Successive waves of reform led to the majority of large hospitals being awarded trust status and a significant number of GPs chose to become fundholders.

The importance of ideas and the triumph of theory

Marmor and Plowden (1991: 812) argue that the acceptance of Enthoven's pro-market ideas, which were largely untested, is 'an instance of almost pure theory being transplanted across an ocean'. Unlike other policy areas, such as the creation of the Child Support Agency, discussed in Chapter 2, or education reforms, examined in Chapter 4, what was transferred was not an established institution or programme; rather Enthoven advocated a set of general ideas and principles about the management of health services and then applied them to the specific setting of the NHS. While some of the ideas did have a concrete existence within the existing American health care system, particularly in the rapidly expanding system of Health Maintenance Organizations (HMOs), with which Enthoven was closely involved, there was no such thing as an 'internal market' in America.

Enthoven the entrepreneur and the health network

The intervention of Enthoven resembles that of policy entrepreneurs who, as Rose emphasizes (1993: 56), are important actors in the transmission of ideas and policies because 'their concern with a special subject . . . leads them to build up a nation-wide or international network of contacts that are a source of ideas for new programs'. From his base at Stanford University, Enthoven was one of the key figures within a network of health economists, who had been successful in making their profession a very visible and influential source of input into the health policy debate around the globe. As Moran argues (1993: 9), 'the fact that the American health care debate is a debate about costs and efficiency is in no small measure due to the ability of health economists to penetrate the policy making networks'. Moreover, the 'immense prestige' of the American health economist at the international level has contributed to the export of American policy innovations as they have headed up an international epistemic community devoted to the spread of their ideas and proposals.

Economic analysis when applied to health care brings a distinctive perspective and raises questions about the role of government in health care; the value of competition; the importance of consumer choice; and a mistrust of the monopoly practices of health providers. Efficiency in the delivery of health care is seen not only as desirable but also as an ethical imperative since wasting resources on one case means losing the opportunity to provide beneficial treatment to other members of society. However, there are many difficulties associated with the application of economic theory to health care which help explain some of the difficulties associated with the internal market. What does consumer choice mean in relation to something as complex and emotive as health care, where knowledge is likely to be imperfect? What about public safety? History suggests that the expansion of state responsibility for health care was largely in response to the threat that diseases, such as cholera, represented to the safety and stability of industrializing societies. The emergence of new diseases like AIDS and the resurgence of old threats such as tuberculosis (TB) highlight the continued importance of public health issues. There are also many technical problems. How does a market distribute health care when demand is unrelated to price? How is price determined in health care? Lastly, there are fundamental questions about the compatibility of market principles with the goals of equity and universal access which are particularly pertinent to the NHS. So, while market-oriented reforms could arguably work in health care systems which have always incorporated market elements, such as choice of which physician is consulted and an equation of medical care with the exchange of money, as is the case in America, such principles are very far removed from the British system. Furthermore, even the language of the market was alien until the arrival of Thatcherism and thus, in a sense, remained shocking to many British ears, particularly in relation to the NHS.

Differences between the two health care systems

The American health care system appears almost incomprehensibly fragmented, diverse and complex to an observer used to the monolithic National Health Service. Furthermore, as a private system based on voluntary insurance, it is also based on very different principles. The idea that, as a visitor to the United States, you are at risk of being left to die on the pavement if you have been foolish enough not to take out health insurance has a mythic quality. This mythic image is often contrasted, in popular journalism, with the 'free' NHS which treats everyone, including visiting Americans if they become ill or injured. However, Americans view British 'socialized medicine' with its lack of choice, waiting lists and austerity as equally undesirable. In fact, one of Enthoven's many criticisms of the NHS was that it is 'frozen by an excess of egalitarianism'. Certainly survey data over the years reveal that Americans wish to make their own choices, even if constrained by the choices presented to them by the HMO to which they belong, rather than have medical relationships overseen by government agencies. Thus, it is 'routinely cited' that the US does not want or need anything like the NHS (Hacker 1997: 26).

The role of institutions and culture

The differences between the two systems go much deeper than organizational characteristics but reflect deep historical and cultural differences. Rosemary Stevens (1984: 189) outlines how the development of professional practice, regulation and medical education took quite different paths in the two countries. More importantly, she stresses how these developments took place alongside general differences in social attitudes towards medical care, which even extended to the behaviour of patients within the two systems. One of the manifestations of such differences has been the contrasting role of money in the British and American health care systems. As long ago as 1893 Henry Burdett was critical of England where 'free relief has now become so general that the majority of the population consider it the most natural thing in the world to . . . demand and receive free medical treatment without question or delay'. This he contrasted with America which 'owing no doubt to the fact of its being a relatively new country, possessing few endowed charities and an energetic population . . . may be regarded as the home of the pay system' (quoted in Stevens 1984: 189). American patients were used to paying for hospital treatment in contrast to the mainly charitable English hospital system. On top of this, patients in England were already characterized as being relatively passive recipients of medical care compared to more 'adventurous and litigious' Americans (p. 189). This is a difference which can still be observed in the patriarchal and deferential relationship which has characterized the encounter between British doctors and their patients. Only slowly does a passive relationship give way to a more challenging one based on principles such as informed consent, which have long been valued in America (Sabin 1992).

Such differences in social attitudes and medical practice have helped to contour the landscape on which the formal system of care is located. Moreover, these differences highlight why the analysis of different organizational structures must account for culturally ingrained beliefs about medical care. This is particularly so when making any assessment of the NHS. The National Health Service is as much an idea as an institution. At the time of its creation the NHS epitomized the collectivism current in post-war Britain. Britain was the first country to offer free medical care to the whole population. Moreover, provision was based not on the insurance principle of entitlement following contributions but rather reflected a collectivist view which saw health as a public good rather than an individual right (Klein 1995: 1). Aneurin Bevan, the architect of the NHS, articulated these impulses when he reflected that 'a free health service is a triumphant example of collective action and public initiative applied to a segment of society where commercial principles are seen at their worst' (1952: 85). Whatever the realities of the subsequent performance, the idea of the NHS as embodying principles of equity, universalism and social solidarity has been remarkably resilient and very popular.

Such principles are largely absent from the American health care system. For example, there is no universal access to health care. Because of this some 40 million adults and children, about 15 per cent of the population, have no health insurance while many others are reliant on 'Swiss cheese' policies, which do not provide comprehensive coverage (Health Policy Network 1996: 9; Hacker 1997: 28). Moreover, unlike other national systems which are based on an insurance model, in the United States health insurance and health coverage has never been seen as a right or a societal obligation; rather it is perceived as a private, voluntary matter.

Most Americans obtain health insurance through a wide variety of workplace-based schemes with varying co-payment levels. Medicaid for the poor and Medicare for the elderly are publicly run schemes but access to Medicaid is highly variable between different states and there is a substantial problem for low-income families who may not qualify for Medicaid assistance but can't afford to buy adequate private cover for themselves and their family. There have been many attempts at structural reform to introduce a system of universal coverage but all, including the recent effort by the Clinton administration, have failed.

Cost containment is also a major problem. Expenditure on health now absorbs over 13 per cent of the American Gross Domestic Product (GDP). This compares to an OECD average of 8.1 per cent (Blank 1997: 129). The problem is that increased spending has not resulted in higher levels of health. For example, in comparison with six other developed nations America ranks seventh in infant mortality and sixth in female life expectancy at birth, though it should be noted that these rates are considerably higher for members of the minority and poor populations (Blank 1997: 130).

In view of these failures, the fact that American ideas about health care have had a persuasive influence on the reform of the NHS is surprising to many observers. Klein (1995: 187) suggests that the influence of American ideas was 'very much a case of experts on obesity advising a patient suffering from anorexia', while the American health care analyst Theodore Marmor expresses his puzzlement as to what, in view of the difficulties with both coverage and cost control, American policy experience can teach others about economy and effectiveness in the delivery of medical care. He argues that the problems associated with American health care should be kept in mind, 'as reports of American success stories with "managed care" and "competition" continue to be distributed widely in the global marketplace of ideas' (Marmor 1997: 350).

The market as a focus for dissent

Although the government continued to reaffirm its commitment to the founding principles of the NHS, the *Working for Patients* reforms were interpreted by many as representing a significant attack on, if not sounding the death knell of, the National Health Service. Different analysts highlight different reasons as to why the *Working for Patients* reforms were so unpopular. The force of protest against the internal market was somewhat surprising considering that Enthoven's proposals had been at least cautiously welcomed by some sections of the medical profession before they were taken up by the government. Klein suggests (1990: 701–2) that exclusion from the review and the policy-making process was the main reason for the bitterness and opposition of the medical profession rather than the review's actual policy content. However, while it is undoubtedly the case that opposition to the reforms had complex origins it was the market-oriented aspects of the reforms which became the most visible and coherent focus of dissent.

The proposed market and the language of contracts, incentives and competition that went with it was seen by many as being particularly alien and destructive to the traditions and values encapsulated within the NHS. While the British public may have been more sanguine about other policy areas, the import of market principles into health care appeared particularly inappropriate and offensive. Opinion polls consistently showed almost three-quarters of voters opposed to the changes, believing that they signified the Conservatives' true intention of privatizing the NHS (Timmins 1995: 470) – a charge that the Labour Party repeatedly asserted. Opposition from the medical profession was also extremely vocal. The British Medical Association (BMA) spent £3 million on an advertising campaign opposing the reforms and called on its members not to cooperate with the government (Timmins 1995: 468). The fear was that the supremacy of medical need would be overridden by considerations of cost and profitability. A BMA pamphlet publicizing its opposition to the reforms asked: 'Do you want the cheapest treatment or what is best for you?' Competition was seen as inappropriate, unnecessary and destructive of professional relations based on trust and dedication. But was it worth the storm? Have the reforms yielded the benefits promised by their architects or confirmed the worst fears of their critics?

The market in practice

Making a reasoned assessment of the impact of the reforms is difficult. There have not been many evaluative research studies and assessment has been hampered by the evolutionary nature of the reform process. One of the most commonly identified failures of the reform strategy concerns the way in which the internal market operated. Maynard (1994: 1437) argues that policy makers did not fully understand the logic of Enthoven's arguments about the use of competition with the result that the 'Thatcher government "lurched" the NHS towards a competitive system but fell far short of achieving this goal'. A number of analysts confirm this view and terms such as 'managed market' or 'quasi-market' are commonly used to indicate that the public services generally, and the health services specifically, are different so that assumptions about the operation of markets simply do not apply (Williams and Flynn 1997: 136). One research project which looked at the impact of contracting on the management of health services across a number of geographical locations concludes that a number of constraints limited the development of a market in health care. One of the most powerful constraints on market principles was the continued importance of localized patterns of service provision. The attachment to locally accessible services meant that few purchasers were willing to destabilize existing arrangements and 'risk the political and public fall-out of threatening local providers' (Spurgeon *et al.* 1997: 152). Another source of tension between market principles and their application to the health sector is in the nature of the relationships between purchasers and providers. Research highlights the continuance of cooperation rather than outright competition. Studies have highlighted the reluctance of purchasers to engage in a 'hard'-style contractual relationship with purchasers and instead outline how space has been left for the continuance of collaborative, mutual relationships (Williams and Flynn 1997: 155). Such findings highlight the gap between the language and politics of the market and the nature of the activities in which those working in health services see themselves as engaged. Another common criticism of the market has been the high transaction costs and an inflated bureaucracy associated with the operation of the highly complex contracting system which critics argue takes resources away from patient care. There are also concerns about equity associated with the alleged emergence of a two-tier system in which the patients of GP fundholders receive preferential treatment. On the other hand, supporters of the reforms have accused the Department of Health of continually interfering in the operation of the internal market which increased central control of the service and stifled the promise of local freedom.

These points highlight how fragile and limited the development of the internal market was. While there have undoubtedly been many changes in health care provision it is hard to detail how many of these changes are a direct result of the internal market and how many are due to other changes inside medicine, such as changing clinical practice, or to other policy initiatives, such as the move towards a primary care-led National Health Service. Moreover, even before the election of the Labour government, committed to abolishing the internal market, in May 1997, the language of the market had largely faded from health policy discourse. For example, *A Service with Ambitions* (DoH 1996), the NHS White Paper published in the last months of the Major government, made no mention of markets and competition. Instead it focused upon the issues of information, staff skills and 'managing for quality' in order to achieve a 'responsive' service. A new, softer language of cooperation and team working has replaced the harsher language of the market and, while the Labour government has opted to retain the separation between purchasers and providers, competition is no longer seen as a viable or desirable way of allocating resources. The White Paper, *The New NHS: Modern, Dependable* (DoH 1997), outlines the Labour government's intention to replace the internal market with a system of 'integrated care' which emphasizes a collaborative approach and partnership between the different sectors of the NHS.

From markets to managed care

While the focus of reform has shifted away from markets and competition there can be no return to the past. The potentially limitless rise in future health care expenditure set against tight public spending constraints means that all governments are concerned to continue to improve the performance of health services without incurring increased costs. The focus is now on the delivery of care and the new buzzword in health care reform is 'managed care'. The central principle behind managed care is an attempt to place controls on the working practices of health professionals, making their work more transparent and easily monitored in terms of cost and quality. Managed care is now a dominant feature of the American health care system. In fact, Anders argues that with the rise of Health Maintenance Organizations, 'managed care has become the de-facto national health policy of the United States' (quoted in Hacker 1997: 26).

Managed care in America evolved during the 1970s and 1980s from the desire of large employers to contain and/or reduce the premium costs of their employees' health insurance premiums. In the traditional 'fee-for-service' system, insured individuals could exercise choice over which doctor or specialist hospital service to use. Insurance companies would then reimburse service providers directly. Since the 1980s insurance companies have taken a much more interventionist strategy. Jointly, with medical providers, they have developed a range of schemes which fundamentally altered the 'fee-for-service' system. Health Maintenance Organizations (HMOs) are the most widespread embodiment of the new principles in action. HMOs combine the functions of insurers and treatment providers in one organizational structure. In return for a fixed 'capitation fee' from each of its members an HMO undertakes to provide a wide range of medical and hospital services. Most HMOs employ doctors on fixed salaries and often have inbuilt performance indicators and incentives for keeping costs down. They also require patients to see a family doctor approved by the HMO, who performs a gatekeeping role for access to more expensive specialist services. As the insurance market place has expanded and grown, more competitive managed care organizations increasingly offer a range of alternative arrangements for their clients. More than half of Americans now receive their health care through some form of managed care scheme, many of them run by for-profit organizations.

The National Health Service already displays some of the features of managed care as they have recently evolved in America. The role of general practitioners, as 'gatekeepers' to specialist hospital-based services, has always been one of the key features of the NHS. Patient choice has also been much less of a central feature than rhetoric would have us believe. It could be argued that the elevation of the primary care 'gatekeeping' role and a reduction in choice represent two of the ways in which the American system is moving closer to the British. It also indicates that there may be a certain amount of convergence between the two systems.

One of the key features of the American development of managed care is the role of competition. As a supporter of the Health Maintenance Organization system Enthoven emphasizes the central role of competition between different HMOs. He used the term 'managed care – managed competition' and argued that it was consumer choice of HMO that provided the incentive for organizations to give value for money (Newman 1995: 1652–5). A second important feature is that the development of managed care in America has been a private sector response and is mainly being pursued by private for-profit insurers. Both these features have been questioned and subject to criticism both within the United States and by European analysts considering the possible applicability of managed care for European health care systems. In the United States there are concerns that HMOs are successfully screening out high-risk patients, making it difficult for individuals with disabilities, chronic illness or high-risk factors, such as a genetic predisposition to illness or AIDs, to obtain comprehensive coverage at competitive rates (Fairfield et al. 1997). Attempts are being made across the US, even at the federal level, to introduce legislation which would place more control over HMO selection procedures. There are also fears that the competitive HMO system acts as a brake on innovation, as it is not clear who will reimburse research and the more experimental end of patient care. In addition, professionals are increasingly expressing concerns about the compatibility of their clinical freedom to diagnose and treat the patients in their best interests with the use of financial incentives designed to keep costs down. Critics also argue that the consumer choice is purely rhetorical, as most insured Americans have to accept the plans that their employers have installed, making it impossible to move to an HMO of their liking or out of the HMO system altogether (Blank 1997). Finally, it is worth stressing once again that there is no choice for the millions of individuals who lack medical insurance and thus fall into the vagaries of the public system.

However, many of these criticisms are connected to the nature of the American health system. When it comes to the actual techniques of managed care at a micro level the evidence is more mixed. In particular, European advocates of managed care argue that, in the context of a publicly funded and publicly provided health care system, managed care may have a contribution to make. Unlike the internal market which, as has been argued here, was alien and ran contrary to the ethos of the National Health Service, managed care, shorn of its American connection with competition and profit, appears less threatening and has the potential to change the delivery of care substantially (Hollamby 1995).

There is a lot of professional interest in the techniques of managed care and the Department of Health has also shown a long-standing interest in the development of HMOs. Civil servants from the Department of Health have been to America to study HMOs. In 1995 the Department of Health sponsored a group of individuals working in purchasing, the Leaders in Purchasing Group, to look at US developments in Managed Care (UK Lip Service Group Report 1995). Although there is as yet no official emphasis on managed care as a policy objective within the NHS, the techniques associated with it look set to assume a greater importance in future policy debates. Fairfield and her colleagues argue that the time is right to move the debate about managed care further into the public arena (Fairfield et al. 1997). Hopefully policy makers will take the opportunity to look at the negative as well as positive lessons from American experience before policy is developed. Crucially, ideas about managed care need to be translated into the British context if the kind of upheaval that followed the introduction of the internal market is to be avoided.

Conclusion

The case of the internal market illustrates a number of interesting points about the process of policy transfer. Perhaps most instructive is the way the case highlights the central importance of the domestic context into which ideas and policy innovations from abroad are imported. Health care systems are deeply rooted in the institutional, political and social circumstances of an individual country. This is particularly important when considering the National Health Service which has emerged as a very important institution within the British political and cultural structures. Klein argues that 'the test of any model of health care is its appropriateness to a particular setting' and that 'real learning . . . is about *distinguishing*, about knowing when a particular model is relevant or irrelevant to the specific circumstances of a country' (1997: 1269, emphasis in original). To many people competition and markets appeared both inappropriate and irrelevant for the British NHS. Putting aside the operational difficulties encountered with the actual running of the internal market, the new discourse of competition contracts and cost-efficiency that was injected into health care debates in the late 1980s came to symbolize the inevitable and unwanted 'Americanization' of the NHS. This contributed to the highly charged atmosphere surrounding the announcement of the *Working for Patients* reforms and fostered a more generalized atmosphere of discontent and mistrust towards the Thatcher government's intentions for the NHS.

But the importance of the domestic context in the process of transfer is not confined to issues of the compatibility and appropriateness of a particular piece of policy. It also includes a whole range of other, predominantly domestic, considerations. Thus, while American ideas provided an important inspiration for British policy makers, the reason why they were attractive and the exact process by which these ideas were combined with 'home-grown' innovations is very much associated with domestic politics and the particular problem that the NHS represented to the Conservative government as Mrs Thatcher entered her third term of office. Marmor suggests that in most cases policy makers do not seriously consider the lessons from the experiences of other countries and that policy debates are mainly national affairs. He argues: 'when cross-national comparisons are employed in such parochial struggles, their use is typically that of policy warfare, not policy understanding and careful lesson-drawing'

(1997: 361). Marmor's argument does seem particularly pertinent to this case. The reasons why reform was embarked upon; the nature of the review process, including why American ideas were attractive; the content of the *Working for Patients* reforms, which comprised a number of elements and not only American ideas; the opposition to the reforms and the implementation problems that followed reveal as much about the politics of health care in Britain as they provide a clear illustration of policy transfer in action.

There are limits to what can be transferred from other countries in an area such as health policy, which has become not only highly politicized but is also deeply embedded within the national system. Klein (1997) suggests that policy learning in practice is not about the transfer of ideas or techniques, but about their adaptation to local circumstances. It seems reasonable to suggest that the Conservative government may have faced less opposition and implementation difficulties if the reforms had been more appropriately adapted to suit the NHS. The Blair government has kept some of the key changes, notably the purchaser/provider split, but has distanced its policy from that of the previous administration by 'abolishing' the internal market. As was briefly discussed, managed care now appears to be going through a process of adaptation to suit European health care systems.

A second point that the case illustrates concerns who is involved in transfer. The role of Enthoven as a policy entrepreneur, along with the various think tanks and academic forums which developed and publicized the ideas associated with markets and competition in health care, provides an interesting example of the importance of such actors in the international spread of ideas. The fact that it was largely ideas that were being promoted is a third interesting feature of the transfer process. The case of the internal market is an unusual one in terms of the policy transfer model in the sense that the 'market' was from the beginning an abstraction based on a set of ideas rather than an established public policy or institution which had some material existence. But even so these ideas had largely been developed in the context of the American system which operated on entirely different principles to the British NHS. The inherent differences between the two systems played a large part in creating the difficulties outlined above. The case illustrates the fact that ideas can play as large a role as institutions or specific policy instruments in policy transfer, and furthermore that ideas are strongly attached to political and social systems, and thus cannot always be successfully transferred into foreign systems.

As can be seen with the present developments in managed care, the sheer volume and high level of exchange about health care means that policy transfer will continue to play a role in health care reform, although there does seem to be an awareness that the techniques associated with this latest trend need to be put into a domestic context if they are to succeed. In particular policy makers need to understand the limits of policy transfer and take notice of the cultural, historical and political nature of health care systems. Change has more chance of succeeding and carrying the support of those most affected by reform if this is taken on board.

4

Education: post-compulsory education in England and Wales

Rob Hulme

Education has been at the forefront of the political agenda since the mid-1980s. In fact, the New Labour government has proclaimed education reform to be a metaphor for its project to modernize Britain's social and economic structures. Yet, Labour's definitions of educational problems and the responses they have chosen are not new. Indeed, the Labour government's policies demonstrate a distinct lack of originality. Policy towards schools reveals a remarkable degree of inheritance from the previous Conservative government and many of the ideas underlying the proposed restructuring of post-compulsory education have been borrowed from other countries, particularly the United States. The domestic and international iteration of policy in education is a growing phenomenon and one which is in need of further exploration.

The role of policy transfer in changing education policy

This chapter examines the role of policy transfer in the development of British education policy in three ways. First, it examines the role policy transfer played in the changes to primary education over the past fifteen years. This section argues that policy makers turned to policy transfer, primarily from the United States, because they perceived it as being rational to seek tried and tested solutions to the problems faced by the education state instead of trying to generate new and untested policies. In addition to borrowing actual policies and programmes this section will demonstrate that policy makers turned to policy transfer in an attempt to learn how to bring about their ideological 'versions of the truth' in education. Accordingly, it will be argued that the making of education policy tends to be more a process of recycling old ideas and even those of political opponents than genuine innovation. Second, the chapter will examine the interaction of policy transfer and the policy-making process. Here it will be demonstrated that policy transfer can expand our understanding of the 'stages' education policy must travel through on its way to implementation. Third, the chapter examines the role played by transferred ideas and instruments in one of the most significant areas of education policy during the past fifteen years: the expansion and reform of further and higher education from the late 1980s to the Dearing Review in 1997.

The why and how of policy transfer in primary education

The policy transfer framework has provided the necessary connections in a number of areas of education policy which were in need of attention. First, all recent policy change in education has involved the movement of policy ideas and instruments from one context to another. The policy transfer framework provides some insights into how and why this happens. Second, the policy transfer framework helps address some of the uncertainties in the literature on policy learning. It helps identify the nature of 'new' information, where it comes from, who supplies it and the uses to which it is put. Third, policy transfer helps explain the role of ideology in the policy-making process, at least in part, in the search by policy makers for tried and tested responses which will bring about their core ideological goals.

Policy transfer as rational and ideologically driven policy making

A brief examination of the significant changes in the educational state since the mid-1980s reveals that policy transfer played a central role in the 'great education reform' movement which culminated in the 1988 Education Reform Act (ERA) and the 1992 Further and Higher Education Act. Policy sociologists, such as Ball, 'established' that the most dynamic factor of the Conservative education reform policy was ideology: specifically, the interaction of two ascendant, yet contradictory, educational ideologies, cultural restorationism and new vocationalism. However, it must be stressed that the discourses they generated were only effective when they were in accord with wider social and economic movements, such as shifts in the international labour market; the impact of policy from other areas, notably employment; and changes in the balance of power within the policy subsystem. It was such a convergence of factors which stimulated policy makers to begin searching for a change in the general direction of policy in the late 1980s. Briefly, Britain's lack of response to the global skills revolution presented compelling reasons for change, and the large Conservative election victory in 1987 provided the context for the creation of new bodies and actors, such as the new post-compulsory education funding quangos, necessary to force the pace of change.

Interestingly, in education reform, policy transfer almost always involves a combination of voluntary and coercive elements. Policy makers' concern in voluntarily seeking 'new' knowledge from other contexts is to locate policy ideas, symbols and mechanisms which are compatible with their ideological perspective. On the other hand, they are coerced into responding to changing social, economic and political circumstances. These changes often 'force' policy makers to engage in policy transfer as it seems rational to borrow policies other political systems have used to deal with these changes.

In this case, then, policy transfer is both a rational and an ideological strategy to deal with changing circumstance. Seeking workable, tried and tested, readily available definitions and responses from other countries and from the past is in some ways a search for the truth but it is also the politics of the possible. Lessons about a mass post-compulsory education system were transferred from America because, as Sabatier and Jenkins-Smith put it, 'such learning is instrumental' in attaining ideological objectives (1993: 19). Equally, the government was compelled to act by the need for a better skilled workforce.

Policy transfer and fundamental change in education

Truly fundamental change involving major disturbances in the political, economic and social parameters of British education is rare and takes considerable time to achieve. The platform of legislative reform of the late 1980s and early 1990s had its origins in the challenges to the British state presented by movements in the global economy from the mid-1970s. Such changes presented new problems, such as the skills shortage, to which policy makers did not have readily available responses. Almost simultaneously, the political balance of forces was disturbed in the rise of the New Right and the Conservative victory in 1979. These shifts challenged the 'fundamental core values' of the previously dominant coalitions within the educational state, resulting in their destabilization and reformation. Reformed coalitions, with an intellectual leadership drawn from: New Right think tanks, such as the Hillgate Group and the Institute for Economic Affairs; in figures such as Caroline Cox and Stuart Sexton (Ball 1994); and from rising epistemic communities in education, were all instrumental in redrawing the education policy agenda and producing policy prescriptions to match the new political project. The close relationship between the dominant ideological groups or coalitions and epistemic communities facilitated the prerequisite of major change. The process of moulding and then disseminating the knowledge of these groups and actors was assisted by the replacement of key actors within the educational bureaucracy, such as the appointment of cultural restorationist Brian Griffiths to the National Curriculum Council

(Chitty 1989), and later the appointment of Chris Woodhead to head the Schools Inspectorate.

The importance of transfer in the process of making and changing education policy can be captured in the maxim that there is 'nothing new under the sun'. Innovation is almost completely absent in a process involving the frequent recycling, redefinition and reconstitution of policy ideas and instruments from the past, from other countries and from opposing ideological projects or political parties. The location from which policy is sought depends on the balance of forces referred to above and on the immediate needs of policy makers. There is a time at which policy makers will seek suitable policy ideas. This moment involves a convergence in political and economic circumstance with the building of ideological coalitions and policy platforms. The brevity of this moment increases the likelihood that policy makers will seek tried and tested solutions to problems rather than develop new policies and programmes.

However, this must be tempered with the knowledge that in education policy the equation of poor educational standards with progressive teaching methods has become overly familiar. Kingdon (1995) suggests that we ought to expect this: 'This familiarity is the logical outcome of the (policy) processes. If alternatives change not by mutation but by re-combination, there will always be familiar elements in the re-combination' (p. 141). In this respect the most recent education reform has involved the reconstitution of very old themes with newer ideas and mechanisms transferred from other countries. Kingdon observes the frequency of such phenomena in the construction of any policy agenda:

> Proposals may not come back in the same form; rather they are recast, combined with something else or attached to a problem different from the one they started with. After a subject has been through the lengthy gestation period of most major issues, the alternatives become familiar, the options narrow to a few well-understood possibilities, and a limit is reached on the ability to introduce new material.
>
> (pp. 141–2)

Yet what marks recent education reform as exceptional in this respect is the extent to which the transfer of policy ideas from the past has been a central objective of policy. Those moulding the discourses of policy have plundered Britain's and other nations' pasts in search of ideas suited to the political project of reform. In opposing progressivism and the comprehensive system, cultural restorationist actors, such as the Hillgate Group, have transferred as symbolic ideals models of education from the domestic past, in particular the structures and curricular practices of 1950s grammar schools. These ideas have been (and still are) used in generating what Ball (1994) refers to as a 'discourse of derision' about the comprehensive system: the drive to 'improve standards' through the reintroduction of selection and diversity in the school system. Ball observes the extent to which the recent educational past is transferred in the process of policy advocacy in both positive and negative ways:

An imaginary past of national glories and civilising influence is to serve as model and guardian for the future . . . The neo-Conservatives see their role on the one hand in the mobilisation of pasts which can be accepted approvingly and on the other, in the mobilisation of those pasts which would only provoke criticism and rejection.

(Ball 1994: 6)

The transfer of symbolic policy objectives from the domestic past has been central to the reform of Britain's system of education from schools to the post-compulsory sector.

The interaction of policy transfer and the educational reform process

Transfer then, as Wolman (1992) observes, is an integral part of the policy-making process. Knowledge, transferred from other contexts and repackaged for different purposes, is evident throughout the policy process in education, from problem definition and agenda construction stages through to the actual implementation of a policy.

Problem definition and agenda construction

In defining problems and constructing the institutional agenda, policy makers may at first be guided by their ideological predispositions, but these are impure. As Haas (1990: 8) observes 'the knowledge available about a problem determines definitions and possible responses'. In the processes of problem definition epistemic communities help supply policy makers with the 'new' knowledge they need to adapt their views. Haas has characterized this process as the 'unpacking of problems and re-packaging of them in different patterns'. In interpreting problems, epistemic communities inevitably draw on the experiences of many countries and the past. Or, as Haas reminds us 'commonly experienced problems seem to invite the comparison of new solutions' (1990: 44).

The transfer of general policy objectives from other countries is, therefore, common during policy makers' efforts 'correctly' to define the problem they are addressing. This is because policy makers seek out cause–effect prescriptions from polities with a compatible history of problems and preferred solutions. Interestingly, education policy makers often seek to transfer symbolic justifications of their policy proposals rather than actual policies or programmes. This frequently involves 'repackaging' or remoulding the problem and the response; 'filtering-out' those elements of past practice or policy from other countries not in accord with current political priorities. Thus, it will be shown that British policy makers were, and still are, eager to find definitions and responses to the skills shortage among young people and models of mass higher education from the US, Australia and other countries which fit the policy blueprint.

Policy formulation

The input of new or reconstituted knowledge into the policy process is not limited to the definition of problems. Policy transfer, particularly international transfer, is common in the selection of instruments. There is increasing evidence of an international market in policy responses from which policy makers and the analytical actors involved in formulation can choose 'second-hand' instruments. The internationalization of epistemic communities is assisting this burgeoning iteration of policy making in education and training. What policy makers seek is a quick and cheap response to complex problems. For example, the decision to import an American-style education market for post-compulsory education led to the selection of the American model of top-up loans when formulating a means of financing expansion (McFarland 1993). The failure of the US private sector loan model led to almost immediate policy review.

Policy transfer plays an integral part in the politics of formulation. Robertson (1991: 75) highlights the importance of transfer in the process of political and ideological conflict: 'People fight with ideas as well as about them . . . Policy-makers use lessons as instruments of power to gain leverage in political conflicts. Lessons from other states can advance the case for change.' Transferred policy goals, symbols and instruments are used by coalitions as weapons in the process of conflict with other groups. This is so, whether the coalitions are proponents or opponents of change and accordingly whether the transferred 'tool' is put to positive/constructive or negative/deconstructive use.

A related aspect of transfer is the extent to which policies are transferred across the political spectrum in the politics of policy formulation. Policy knowledge is a resource in the struggle for ideological dominance and if a policy idea is seen to be working for others, it can be remodelled to serve a different ideological purpose. In education in particular, a growing phenomenon of gradual assimilation of apparently opposing political ideas has become apparent.

The evolution of Labour's education policy from the mid-1980s to the present is an interesting case in cross-coalition transfer. In the case of comprehensive schooling, this took the form of the incremental acceptance of 'choice and diversity' in the type of schooling offered, the adoption of more radical restorationist platforms on grammar schools, the acceptance of the gradual re-introduction of selection and the individualization of performance management in schools. Labour's emerging 'neo-restorationism' is taking an interesting new turn in developing a neo-liberal flavour in policy proposals intended to encourage 'partnerships' between public and private schools. The continuity of transferred policy and the establishment of the ideas of cultural restorationism under the New Labour government has been underlined by its endorsement of Chris Woodhead, the Chief Inspector of Schools, the former standard bearer of neo-conservatism in schools. If this approach is to be continued, the effect will be to remix the uneasy policy formula of the previous government in a slightly different package.

Implementation

Policy transfer in the process of implementing education institutions is less common than the transfer of ideas and symbols and appears to be much more likely to fail. The political, cultural and administrative specificity of education systems determines that the transfer of specific institutions and mechanisms is fraught with difficulty. However, the practical politics of change in education is about reinforcing or breaking systems of control; this requires careful control of the actors in the networks. There have been attempts, therefore, to transfer implementing agents or mechanisms, particularly for the task of managing and controlling change by stabilizing or breaking down various implementation networks. This is a crucial aspect of change for, as Sabatier (1988, 1991) observes, policy will not change until the actors sustaining dominant coalitions have been replaced. An example of this type of change can be seen in the Thatcher government's use of quangos to bring about market reforms in further and higher education.

The time involved in transfer

It should be clear that the making of education policy is a fluid and evolutionary process, involving struggle and compromise at every stage and level. Policy does not emerge from the policy process at any stage with a fixed meaning. Rather, it continually changes its meaning while on its journey towards implementation. Major reform, such as that begun in the British education system during the late 1980s and early 1990s, particularly the expansion of the system of post-compulsory education, can take a decade or even a generation to implement. Time is needed for the realignment of political alliances, the acquisition of key posts by advocates and brokers and for new knowledge about the nature and scope of policy problems to permeate political debate and the policy-making process. Thus, transferred knowledge can take many years to enter the policy process. On this journey it is often reshaped by advocates in a political debate, or completely disappears only to emerge in a reconstituted, sometimes unrecognizable, form.

Ideas originally transferred from the US in the 1970s, such as a national curriculum in schools and the idea of an educational market, tended to surface in neo-liberal think tanks, like the Institute of Economic Affairs (IEA). Moreover, many of the ideas borrowed from the United States during this time were only partly formed, gestating within numerous think tanks, which acted as both advocate and expert, tailoring them to the needs of Conservative politicians. Interestingly, other ideas transferred into the policy debate, such as the education voucher for schools, did not materialize in the Conservatives' platform of reform.

The increasing evidence of iteration in the policy process in education (i.e. the Dearing Review) provides evidence that policy transfer can be creative, marking a break with policy makers' predisposition to continuity. However, even with this incremental learning process it must be stressed that policy transfer often leads to policy failure. In education, policy makers tend to engage in partial transfer because they are often looking for a justification for a policy platform or a 'quick fix' solution. Education systems are products of national cultures and any attempt to 'borrow' parts of them is likely to end in implementation failure, particularly given the close-knit nature of British education networks and the complexity of the educational state.

Policy transfer in the reform of post-compulsory education in England and Wales in the 1980s and 1990s[23]

The Education Reform Act of 1988, the Higher Education Reform Act of 1991 and the Further and Higher Education Act of 1992, along with intermediary legislation, had the effect of transforming the system from an elite to a mass basis by tripling the numbers in both sectors (DES 1991a). While these Acts transformed the British education system during the 1980s and 1990s, in formulating them the British government actively transferred policies from the United States. For example, the American notion of normalizing full-time education to 18 and mass participation in higher education was transferred as a policy goal, as was the basic model of a marketization in higher education, mirroring in many respects the competitive market for schools. Policy mechanisms to facilitate the operation of the market were also 'borrowed', student loans and, through 'incorporation', certain organizational forms and management techniques for colleges and universities were also transferred.

Policy makers were drawn to the United States because changes in Britain's competitiveness in the global economy prompted action and the US offered a model of educational expansion compatible with the government's ideological perspectives and goals. As such, the reform of the British post-compulsory education system provides a classic example of policy transfer. More importantly, it provides an illustration of not only a hybrid piecing together of policy reform but is a case in which both voluntary and coercive forces acted together to convince policy makers to act. The debate about policy change was shaped by broad-based coalitions of interest advocating new vocationalism and, to a certain extent, new progressivism. These ideas were also represented by key analytical actors such as Her Majesty's Inspectorate (HMI) and the Committee of Vice-Chancellors and Principals (CVCP) active within the 'epistemic communities' shaping the debate on the nature of policy. Equally evident, at all levels, was the cultural restorationist resistance to change; resistance which had shaped policy in the past and resulted in significant reshaping and 'filtering' of transferred policy.

The transformation of post-compulsory education, though, is not simply a one-dimensional process of appropriation from the US. The shape and character of the post-16 educational state was also determined by ideas transferred from

Britain's history of educational policy making. Ending the binary divide and the process of 'massification' represented in many ways the delayed fulfilment of the Robbins Report (DES 1963) from 30 years earlier.

The government sought to transfer elements of the US system in order to achieve an easily controllable, expanded system at the least cost. Thus, what was not transferred has been as significant as what was transferred in the reform of the system. The transfer of parts of the US system and their reconstitution within a 30-year-old model of higher education inevitably produced anomalies and problems leading ultimately to the Dearing Review's pessimistic evaluation of the system in 1997. Interestingly, the review is underpinned by information transferred from other countries, notably the United States and Australia, and represents (perhaps) the complete importation of the American higher education system started in the late 1980s.

Why did British policy makers look to America?

By the late 1980s the system of further and higher education was perceived by the Thatcher government as being incapable of delivering students competent to function in the new 'Post-Fordist' economy. Thus, the primary reason for action was the perception within both the new vocationalist lobby and the more progressive-orientated professional lobby that Britain was failing to respond to the challenges presented by transitions in the global economy. The problem was that British industry was beginning to fall behind its international competitors particularly in the US, Germany and Japan (Esland 1991). Further and higher education had to be restructured in order to supply the demand for a generation of young people possessing flexible polyvalent skills for the emergent Post-Fordist economy (Finegold et al. 1992a).

Britain's lag in the global skills revolution presented a two-fold problem for the system of post-compulsory education. First, the lack of participation of 16- to 18-year-olds. Raffe and Rumberger (1993) indicate that in 1990 only 50 per cent of 16-year-olds stayed in full-time education, with only 20 per cent going on to full-time education beyond 18. More disturbing to policy makers was the fact that despite the doubling of the further education population in the period 1985–95 to 57.3 per cent, and the trebling of the post-18 population in higher education to 33 per cent, the OECD still ranked Britain third from the bottom for participation in post-secondary education (Times Educational Supplement, 10 November 1995). Second, and inseparable from the participation issue, policy makers perceived the country as suffering from a 'low-skills equilibrium' (Finegold et al. 1992a). This arises because the education system tends to encourage academic specialization for a small percentage of young people while discouraging the majority of low-achieving young people from either entering higher education or seeking further education and training outside the formal classroom setting.

Allied to this was the need to create a new type of education system for the post-welfare state. The expansion of further and particularly higher education in the post-war period has been closely tied to the political management of the welfare state (Finegold, *et al.* 1992a; Scott 1995). The last significant period of expansion in higher education took place in the 1960s in response to the 1963 Robbins Report (DES 1963). This report sought to develop a national system of post-compulsory education through the 'nationalization' of the polytechnics and colleges. While the report did not lead to the universalization of the education system it did lead to an increase in participation from 8 per cent in 1963 to 13 per cent in 1981 (Scott 1995: 5).

During the 1980s, Conservative governments, fuelled by neo-liberal ideology and prompted by the problems indicated above, sought to develop the ideological and institutional foundations of the post-welfare education state. The political strategy was founded on the perceived need for efficiency and the superiority of the market over state planning. Thus, the government engendered a 'new managerialism' in public services, through the creation of 'quasi-markets'. In the educational state, the introduction of the market meant contracting out and the development of a new consumerism, backed up by audit.

In the post-compulsory sector, this approach was distinct for a number of reasons. First, the contradictions inherent in such an approach to public policy were particularly pronounced on education. New vocationalist elements of the Conservatives' education project wished to realize a modern system which was responsive to the economy. Neo-conservative cultural restorationists, however, were keen to establish control of the sector but extremely reluctant to oversee the abandonment of the 'meritocratic elitism' of the university system. 'Marketizing' post-compulsory education therefore meant an abandonment of the government's duty to provide higher education for the purpose of social justice, or indeed economic efficiency. Managerialism was therefore to be accompanied by the creation of new structures for self-government.

The government looked to the United States for policy responses because the US was facing comparable problems and could be relied upon for ideological and political parity. While the United States was facing similar structural problems in response to global change there were considerable differences in terms of its manifestation in the system of post-compulsory education. In addition to the structural changes occurring in both the US and the UK, America had a need to respond to the new market for flexible labour thus, as Raffe and Rumberger observe, the problem was inverted: where Britain had a 'staying on problem,' America had a 'drop out problem' (1993: 137).

In the United States participation rates were at a level that Britain aspired to. In 1986 nine in ten Americans went on to the equivalent of further education and more than eight in ten stayed beyond the age of 17. An influential HMI report observed, with some admiration, the participation rates in post-compulsory education in the US: '55% of 18–19 year olds, 33% of 20–21 year olds, 18% of 22–24 year olds and 9% of those aged 25–29 years were involved in some form of education' (DES 1989: 3). The main focus in the participation debate in the US is in the equivalent age range to further education in Britain:

the high school drop out rate for 16- to 18-year-olds. Within the 'schooling to adulthood model operating in America, 50% drop out rate in higher education is regarded as acceptable' (McFarland 1993). Equally important, as Raffe and Rumberger (1993) comment, the debate in the US addresses broader issues, such as the purpose of education beyond 16 years of age, with a focus on those groups least represented in the system, particularly ethnic minorities, where drop out rates are highest.

Throughout the 1980s the administrations of Reagan and Bush followed programmes of public sector reform similar to those pursued by the Thatcher governments. The reform movement was underpinned by shared assumptions about the proper role and function of welfare and similar interpretations of the state's role in solving these problems. Such ideological compatibility assisted in the establishment of habitual communication of policy ideas through established networks throughout the 1980s (Robertson and Waltman 1992).

In the field of post-compulsory education the US and the UK have a shared tradition of voluntarism in their approach toward the provision of training. Moreover, there is a shared view of the market as a viable policy alternative to 'public service education'. However, the 'ideology of the market' (Gewirtz *et al.* 1995) was developed and refined much earlier in the United States than in Britain. In fact it was the ideas of American educational marketers, such as Chubb and Moe, who influenced Mrs Thatcher's efforts to 'deliver' a Hayekian market in education (Kenyon 1998). However, it should be noted that significant differences appeared in both the purpose of the educational market transferred to Britain and the level of control and accountability exercised within it.

In addition to Chubb and Moe there is considerable evidence that transfer was facilitated by knowledge gathered by the networks associated with the post-compulsory education state. This evidence strengthened the arguments of the vocationalist and new progressive lobby for extensive expansion of the post-compulsory education system. In particular, prior to any Thatcher or Major reform information was collected during official visits to the United States. In fact, early in the reform process visits by Her Majesty's Inspectorate produced two seminal reports. Then, two years before the publication of the White Papers *Education and Training for the 21st Century* (DES 1991c) and *Higher Education: A New Framework* (DES 1991a), the DES commissioned a report by Her Majesty's Inspectorate into the structure, funding and content of the American higher education system. While these White Papers were being produced the DES commissioned HMI to produce a second report examining quality control systems in the US. For these reports the Inspectorate was briefed to 'make comparisons between the two systems of higher education and to highlight those features of the United States system which have implications for higher education developments in the United Kingdom' (DES 1989: vii).

The HMI reports found much to commend in the US system, such as: the broadly based curriculum, with its emphasis on skills; the organizational form of US colleges, with their 'responsive structures'; quality assessment; and 'sensitivity' to the needs of the users of further and higher education. Lessons were drawn by policy makers on how to achieve higher participation rates for under-represented groups and on the range and diversity of America's academic and vocational programmes. Significantly, recommendations were made about the possibility and desirability of integrating the structure and content of American junior and community college curricula into the British system. Moreover, the reports drew specific attention to the fact that the modular structures and flexibility found in the American system could be used in Britain to increase access and participation rates. The good news was tempered by negative lessons about wastage figures and the absence of national standards.

Even before the HMI studies policy makers had gathered information on the American education system. In 1987 the Secretary of State for Education, Kenneth Baker, made three visits to the United States with the specific intention of studying the US system of student loans (McFarland 1993). This built upon knowledge gained the previous year when Baker went to Chicago and elsewhere to discuss the operation of the educational market in the inner city and investigate the American system of magnet schools. In fact, it is widely believed that magnet schools were the model Baker used to develop City Technology Colleges, though they do not share the former's commitment to the targeting of resources to underprivileged communities.

A significant role in the interaction of British and American epistemic communities was played by senior university interest groups. For example, there was an informal meeting of the CVCP with the American Council of Education in 1991 to 'exchange perceptions' on the structure, funding and organization of higher education. This meeting clearly assisted in 'the eastward drift of ideas'.[24] Moreover, in common with the HMI, the CVCP's concerns included increasing participation, quality control, access and – significantly for post-transfer evaluation – the US two-plus-two system, whereby students study for two years in a local community college, often leading to 'associate degrees', and complete their degree within two years at the local university. Such informal contact was the basis for regular formalized meetings in the early 1980s.

The internationalization of local networks was also significant in the form of college managers seeking information about new organizational forms (Shackleton 1993). In fact, the establishment of cross-Atlantic links at institutional level has been encouraged by Ministers and operates through professional bodies representing managers (Edwards and Wynch 1993).

What was transferred from the US?

Through the series of legislative reforms referred to above, Britain transferred, at least superficially, a basis for the emulation of the American model of mass higher education, featuring in particular the US notion of an educational market. *Aspects of Higher Education in the United States of America* anticipated legislative change in observing that: 'The United States has led the way in providing a system of mass higher education based on open entry to degree courses more broadly based than those in England' (DES 1989: i).

In another act of prescience, prior to the publication of *Higher Education: a New Framework*, which set the target of 'nearly one in three young people to enter education by the year 2000' (DES 1991a), HMI commented:

> If higher education institutions in England are to achieve the participation levels set by the government they will need to re-orient themselves in new ways to recruit not only more of the 18 year old cohort but also groups currently under-represented such as women and mature students.
>
> (DES 1989: 29)

The government exceeded its own target inside five years. By 1995 the full-time undergraduate numbers had risen to 32 per cent of 18- to 21-year-olds and remained at this level after the government placed a cap on expansion (NCIHE 1997: 11), surpassing the most rigorous definitions of a mass system (Trow 1973). Britain, it seemed, was en route to universalism.

In emulating the US notion of a mass system, there were some attempts to revise the notion of 'higher education'. The modern 'multiversity' (Scott 1995) required open access and modular diversity. In *Aspects of Higher Education in the USA*, the HMI and other professional actors, notably the CVCP, encouraged policy makers to emulate American diversity in the curriculum and embrace modularity as a means of widening and deepening access. They were, however, keener on this than the government who wanted massification without making the changes to the nature and the purpose of the system which cultural restorationists throughout the educational state would have abhorred. The language of the Inspectorate reveals an underlying progressivism which was far removed from the language of policy makers at the time:

> One of the main characteristics of post-compulsory education in America is its diversity. A great variety of colleges and universities offer a wide range of vocational, recreational and leisure programmes of study which serve a wide range of individual needs and aspirations. This, together with the modular nature of many of the programmes on offer and the broad general nature of degree programmes, has made higher education much more accessible to all sections of the population.
>
> (DES 1989: 28)

The 1989 report stimulated interest in the participation rates and flexibility of the two-year community colleges 'which perform similar work to colleges of further education in England' and suggested the coupling of statistics on participation from the English further and higher sectors as an indicator of success. Evidence of the impact of such ideas post-1992, disseminated by government but also by international institutional contact, manifested itself in the growth of 'franchise' or 'partnership' agreements between further education colleges and predominantly the new universities, serving to blur the distinction between the sectors. The Dearing Review encouraged the emulation of cross-sectoral partnerships and has been actively encouraged as a means of reconceiving post-compulsory education by the Labour government on its quest to build the 'learning society' (DfEE 1998a).

In transferring the basis, if not the structures, of the American model, the 1992 legislation set in motion a gradual but ill-defined transformation of the nature of the system. This change is still, post-Dearing, searching for definition and purpose with Labour adopting only part of the report's vision of a mass further and higher education, integrated into a system of lifelong learning. The basic characteristics of the post-1992 system, however, have been the normalization of school and college attendance to 18 followed by the transfer of as many as possible to university in an attempt to create a system founded on the existence of just two groups of young people: trainees or students. True emulation of the American system demands the reversal of the proportions of these groups from a majority of trainees in the early 1980s to a majority of students in the 1990s (Ainley 1994).

The blueprint for the creation of an American educational market, set down in Chubb and Moe's influential text *Politics, Markets and America's Schools* (1990), was implemented with immediate effect through the 1992 legislation. Ending the binary divide and bestowing legal autonomy or incorporation on institutions led to fierce competition between colleges, sixth forms and universities for demand-led funding allocated by the new Higher Education Funding Council for England (HEFCE) and the Further Education Funding Council for England (FEFCE).

A by-product of the import of a pseudo-American market has been the development of new management styles and organizational forms in colleges and universities. The Inspectorate advised institutions to 'look westward' in becoming more 'responsive' in 'determining the mission of institutions . . . The new governing bodies of our further and higher education institutions have much to learn from the American model, for this is based on directions from citizens rather than government' (DES 1989: 27).

In further and higher education, as elsewhere, this ethos has expressed itself in attempts to audit and manage the output of institutions by measuring performance through new Quality Audit (QA) systems. Two of the better known of these mechanisms are the Research Assessment Exercise (RAE) and the punitive recruitment targets set for colleges. One of the unintended consequences of these measures is that the increased competition under which the new market has placed universities has become a critical issue in further and higher education.

Why partial transfer led to major policy evaluation

A number of aspects of the reform of further and higher education were not directly transferred from the US. The transfer of ideas from the past, the incomplete nature of the transfer of American structures and the transformation of these ideas when applied to the British circumstances created the problems which prompted a major evaluation of policy in the Dearing Review.

Updating Robbins for a 'very British market'

The contemporary American notion of mass post-compulsory education was not the only model available to policy makers in the late 1980s. The massification of the system represents the re-emergence of the 1963 Robbins Report (DES 1963). Before Robbins was commissioned to produce a blueprint for expansion, the British system was highly selective; fewer than 8 per cent of 16- to 18-year-olds were enrolled in higher and further education. As such, the pre-Robbins system conformed to Trow's (1973) notion of an elite system. Crosland had briefed Robbins to produce a blueprint for the development of a mass university system.

While the Robbins Report (DES 1963) recommended ways to accomplish Crosland's wishes it was never fully implemented, largely due to the efforts of the University Grants Committee which provided a focus for elitist elements within the higher education policy community. Therefore, the embryonic model of massification emerged as 'an extended elite system' in a binary structure (Scott 1995). While the report led to an increase in participation levels from 8 to 28 per cent, it occurred within the elitism demanded by the university establishment of the 1960s, and which even now characterizes the 'exceptionalism of the British system'. Cultural restorationism as an 'educational ideology' has primarily focused on the schools sector, but dogged resistance to vocational reform in post-compulsory education has been a significant aspect of the project. Resistance to diversification and expansion has been particularly vociferous within institutions, revealing the penetration of these ideas into the collegial practices of university departments.

It is possible to see the renewal of expansion in the late 1980s and early 1990s as the transference of the goals of Robbins into contemporary circumstances, a consolidation of post-war student growth rather than a radical massification on the American model, underpinned by the new public management techniques of consumerism, managerialism and control. In this sense, it represents the end of a thirty-year resistance to expansion and reform, a resistance which had successfully marginalized progressive and vocationalist discourses from debate about the structure and content of higher education. The neo-liberalism of the Conservative government had empowered vocationalist discourses and finally brought about the social, economic and political conditions to sustain a mass higher education system.

It is a great irony, as Scott notes, that the model which was best suited to these new conditions was the original mass model, that of the United States in the 1960s. He notes the distinctiveness of a system characterized by a:

> paradoxical combination of extensive state regulation (the result of multi-layered federal–state–local government) and strong commitment to the market. The American system (*of HE in the 1960s*) was shaped by this

culture. Planned stratification on the one hand; an open market on the other.

(1995: 8, emphasis in original)

The uneasy mixture of neo-liberal economics and neo-conservative control evident in the 1980s and early 1990s had finally prepared Britain for the American multiversity of the 1960s.

Reform was heavily influenced by the American notion of a competitive 'educational market', yet the cultural and administrative specificity of the American system, referred to by Scott, combined with the determination of the Conservatives to pursue their ideological project, meant that a very impure and partial version of the market was transferred. Instead, a 'very British' pseudo or 'quasi-market' has been imposed in education. The absence of the market tradition, long established in the US, meant that the government had to intervene with policies and administrative mechanisms intended to mimic the market. The funding councils for further education, the FEFCE and higher education HEFCE, were created to stimulate the demand side of post-compulsory education. Both bodies were established with a clear brief to operate a system of funding linked to student numbers. In effect, institutions receive a core funding based on a fixed percentage of their previous year's income and bid for further students and courses against other institutions with agreed programme areas.

Other aspects of the US model of the educational market have been 'filtered out' because they were not in tune with the government's ideological project. Ball (1993), comparing US and British markets in schools, finds the UK's market 'far more radical in the application of ideologically driven policy', but in terms of reproducing the American market orthodoxy the 'UK education system is organized as a very strange market indeed' (p. 8). The fundamental difference is that the US market systems in schools and in higher education have significant communitarian commitments to the 'social goals of equality or justice embedded within them' (Ball 1993: 15; see also Chubb and Moe 1990). The Thatcher government rejected this aspect of market reform, despite the praise the HMI gave the system for providing open access to 'groups such as women, blacks, Hispanics and mature students' (DES 1989: 20).

The advent of the 'contract state' (Hambleton 1994) in post-compulsory education, whereby regulatory, budgetary and auditing powers have been delegated to quangos such as the FEFCE, Training and Enterprise Councils (TECs) and quality audit bodies, has served to undermine successful policy transfer further. The delegation of public authority to quangos has allowed the government to sidestep the apparently empowering aspects of the market and to select those elements of the US model which best suit its ideological purposes. The sector has been 'depoliticized' as government has tightened its control of the definition, formulation and implementation of policy through 'contracting out' public authority to unaccountable bodies. Problem definition has been fragmented with policy aimed at individuals rather than generic problems, such as the skills shortage. Removing the linkage of the local and regional networks has marginalized public sector and professional voices which would have been critical of the government's policy. The implementation of reform has been redefined as a largely technical process, wherein sensitive problems such as the changes in terms and conditions of employment in further education are 'dumped' onto unaccountable quangos such as the Colleges Employers' Forum.

The consequences of partial transfer

The highly selective nature of transfer from America produced significant anomalies in the operation of the mass system in England and Wales. Essentially, the problems were twofold: insufficient transfer and importation problems.

Insufficient transfer

By 1995 it had become apparent that government attempts to transfer a cheap and easy version of the educational market, without thought for the structure and purpose of post-compulsory education, were having undesirable consequences. A mass system had been achieved and was almost universally approved as an ongoing policy goal but it had brought a new set of problems. Competition between institutions had produced a massive expansion in student numbers, well over 50 per cent between 1989/90 and 1994/5, outstripping public funding, which had fallen by 25 per cent per student over the same period (CVCP 1995). Consequently, expansion was capped, funding withdrawn for capital expenditure and financial penalties introduced for over-recruitment. In addition, the judicious cautioning of the HMI of the need for a thorough review of the purpose and structures of post-compulsory education, as a precondition for implementation of American structures, had been ignored. Instead, as Finegold *et al.* (1992b) observe, more had been interpreted as 'more of the same'. The existing institutional arrangements for teaching, research and funding were inappropriate for a mass system and this was causing problems in the quality of education delivered.

In 1991, HMI commented that the government's intention to 'increase participation and to give institutions greater responsibility for their own governance, are tending to reduce the differences between higher education here and in America'. The American system, though, 'enjoyed a higher level of funding and has more open access which encourages more participation from a more diverse student body' (DES 1991b: 19). For the American system to operate effectively, greater diversity was required in institutional form. The absence of 'bridging' institutions between further and higher education, like community colleges, was impeding the development of the system and underlining the problems caused by the government's failure to transfer the more equitable aspects of America's system. Professional voices within the higher education community began to be critical of expansion without depth.

Importing problems from the United States

Problems in maintaining and auditing quality are nothing new to American education policy makers. The Inspectorate observed the US administration's anxiety to respond effectively to 'growing national concern about the quality of higher education . . . there is an important lesson here for British quality assurance systems in any moves towards a greater degree of self regulation' (DES 1991b: 22). In the face of increasing concern over the effectiveness of quality assessment systems British policy makers and institutional managers have found themselves in a comparable position. The view that the defining characteristics of an American system is 'strong on quantity and weak on quality' has been imported (Edwards and Wynch 1993). Increasing quantity has brought problems in employment which are familiar to students of the US system. The DfEE's own evidence to the Dearing Commission observed that 'there is a limit to how many extra graduates the economy can absorb' (*Guardian*, 6 February 1997).

Importing the market has had the effect of redrawing the binary divide, in a manner not dissimilar to the US system, whereby 'Ivy League' universities attract the vast majority of research funding. The mechanisms of quality audit have ensured that the majority of research funding is concentrated in the hands of an elite group of universities with a strong research tradition, with the rest largely dependent on student numbers or full time equivalent students (FTEs) drawn from their local communities. Michael Shattock argues that if unchecked by the Labour government, this new 'Ivy League-ism' will have the effect of producing a private sector of top research universities, virtually outside the remit of the state (*Guardian*, 10 March 1998).

Transferring responses to transferred problems

The government's primary response to these problems was to commission Sir Ron Dearing to review higher education, after an earlier investigation into post-16-year-old qualifications. The Dearing Committee's report, *Higher Education in the Learning Society*, was billed as 'the first re-working of higher education since Robbins' (*Guardian*, 22 July 1997). Such a claim is an overstatement for a review which was desperately overdue. Had it been commissioned in 1989, the problems involved in implementing expansion might have been avoided. Dearing's recommendation that expansion be renewed and diversity introduced confirms and renews the process of Americanization begun a decade earlier. It is founded on a good deal of transferred evidence gathered on visits to the US, France, Germany, Holland, Australia and New Zealand and it revisits some familiar themes concerning the higher participation rates of the US system, particularly at sub-degree level. 'The UK must plan to match the participation rates of other advanced nations: not to do so would weaken the basis of national competitiveness' (NCIHE 1997: 13, 27).

Further expansion, therefore, has been recommended to levels within 5 per cent of the US, 'from the present 32 per cent to a national average of

45 per cent or more' (Section 29). Echoes of earlier studies are evident in the suggestion that government 'should have a long-term strategic aim of respond-ing to increased demand for higher education, much of which we expect to be at sub-degree level' (Section 29). Consequently, funding increases should be prioritized for those institutions which can demonstrate a commitment to the widening of participation, particularly 'from socio-economic groups II to V, people with disabilities and specific ethnic minority groups' (Section 29).

These recommendations represent the most strident move to date to replicate the American community college model (*Guardian*, 29 October 1996; 26 November 1996). In October 1996, the Commission dispatched a four-strong team to the east coast of the United States with a specific brief to invest-igate the adaptability of the four-year two-plus-two system. The findings of this review are evident in Dearing's suggestion that expansion could focus on the sub-degree level, in higher certificates or diplomas. A form of such sub-degree level course had been offered for many years in some 'new universities' in the guise of Business and Technical Education Council (BTEC) courses. Ironically though, increased competition between institutions during the 1990s, com-bined with the overwhelming demand for degrees among the new intake and concurrent developments in national vocational qualifications (NVQs), has led to a dramatic decrease in demand for such courses, with many universities running down their provision of BTEC courses. Had the recommendation been made ten years earlier, it might have been a realizable goal.

Dearing's most eagerly awaited recommendations concerned funding, and the aspects of transfer within them are significant. Expansion had left a 'tick-ing time bomb for the Treasury' (*Guardian*, 2 September 1997), in that a mass system had been created without a means of funding. The attempt, in 1990, to merge the US-style student loan scheme with the existing grants system had failed. The scheme was seen to be inequitable, inefficient and very costly to the public purse. Dearing's considerations of comparable systems entailed the search for an acceptable means of introducing student contributions to fees. The Commission examined the Australian Higher Education Contribution Scheme, introduced there in 1989, involving a contribution of around 20 per cent of university costs, paid back as a lump sum or through an income tax surcharge of 2–4 per cent (NCE 1993). Drawing on this model and others, Dearing recommended that students contribute £1000 towards fees but that means-tested grants should be retained; any loan scheme introduced by gov-ernment should be income-contingent and linked to future earnings. The report's most significant antipodean lesson, though, was that any loan scheme should be treated separately within public sector accounts. With this measure, Dearing appeared to have found a transferable solution to a transferred problem which could count on the support of actors in the educational state ranging from the CVCP to the National Union of Students and free up the money necessary to expand further education (*Guardian*, 2 September 1997).

In this respect, Dearing's most significant role may be that of entrepre-neur or broker both before and after the May 1997 general election and the publication of the Commission's report in July 1997. When gathering evidence from domestic and foreign sources, the Dearing Commission was careful to involve representatives of every significant interest in post-compulsory education. Largely as a consequence of this, Dearing's recommendations have been the basis for the growth of a new broadly based coalition, supportive of expansion and reform. The new consensus bridges long-standing divisions between vocationalist, progressive and traditional elements of the educational state. Such accord may finally bring about the conditions to complete a thirty-year process of transfer in educational reform.

Since Labour's election victory the process of implementing the Dearing recommendations has been extremely slow, leading Dearing to criticize vocally the Blair government's handling of the report. Within this Dearing has been particularly critical of the government's departures from his prescriptions, particularly in abolishing maintenance grants while ignoring his proposal to introduce a flat rate fee. The Green Paper, *The Learning Age* (DfEE 1998a), has been criticized by Dearing and other advocates of change for its caution and lack of imagination in seeking funding from employers and the City to meet the cost of renewed expansion and widened participation he had recommended. Many of the Commission's foreign lessons though, on the expansion of sub-degree level courses and the need for a national higher education framework, underpinned by a US-style credit accumulation and transfer scheme, have been endorsed (*Times Higher Education Supplement*, 27 February 1998).

The process of policy transfer between the United States and Britain in post-compulsory education shows no sign of abating. In power, Labour has been inspired by the Democrats' approach to post-compulsory education in adopting a unified approach to the further and higher education sectors in its commitment to 'lifelong learning'. This has had an immediate effect in the formulation of policy designed to establish individual learning accounts, a development which mirrors President Clinton's initiative to provide two years of higher education for all Americans (*Times Higher Education Supplement*, 1 August 1997).

Conclusion

Major changes in the direction of education policy, such as that experienced in Britain from the late 1980s, are brought about by the convergence of changing ideological agendas and disturbances to the social, economic and political stability of the subsystem. In such circumstances, policy makers perceive it as rational to seek an ideologically suitable policy or instrument which has been tried and tested in other contexts. The act of policy transfer, then, provides us with a means of understanding the mechanics of policy change; policy makers are putting into effect the knowledge available within the global arena and from the past in realizing their policy goals. In education, this does not involve a simple process of appropriation.

The reform of the system of post-compulsory education in the UK demonstrates the complexity of policy transfer's role in education policy change and the extent to which it can produce contradictory and flawed policy. The expansion of the system involved multiple transfer: institutional forms and structures were transferred not only from the modern US system but also from Britain's and America's past. These ideas were 'filtered' and reshaped in a domestic context. The complexity of transfer in this case reflects the clash of educational ideologies and the long-standing coalitions who espouse them in the educational state. Educational conservatives sought to 'learn' from the past how to extend an elite system, while vocationalists and progressives sought long-term modernization by bringing about an 'American market'. The post-1992 system was a hybrid of the two models, embodying the tensions between these ideas and partiality of transfer. The Dearing Report represents an attempt to resolve these tensions through skilful policy brokerage. The new Labour government may regret any further attempt to side-step Dearing's 'transferred lessons' in adapting the post-compulsory system for the twenty-first century.

5

Law and order: the electronic monitoring of offenders

Mike Nellis

It's coming to America first, the cradle of the best and the worst . . .
Leonard Cohen (1992)

It has been said by David Downes (1997) that the United States is the penal workshop of the world, the place where new ideas and new practices in criminal justice are pioneered, and then exported to, forced upon, or borrowed by, other countries. Britain has been particularly influenced by American policies and programmes because of its common language, similar legal system and in part the common ideological outlook of their governing officials. The link has been especially strong in the post-war period, the era of the 'special relationship' between the two countries, but it is not new (see Radzinowicz and Hood 1986: 376–83). In fact, when one looks closely, one sees that the trade has every once in a while been two-way, rarely uncritical, often mutual, and has occasionally resulted in a mingling of ideas such that it ceases to be clear where something originated and where it was transferred.[25] It must also be noted that in the late nineteenth and early twentieth centuries there were strong links between criminologists and criminal justice policy makers in Britain and other European countries, as well as with America. So, even though there are fewer instances of the British government importing or *adapting* practice from Europe, it does happen. For instance, Forsythe (1990: 34) notes that Sir Evelyn Ruggles-Brise, a notable Chairman of the English Prison Commission, 'was an ardent enthusiast for the critical study of foreign penal systems both in America and Europe and from 1895 onwards he represented his country at the quinquennial International Penitentiary Congresses held in various capital cities, being president of the executive body overseeing these congresses from 1910 to 1926'. There were even contacts before this, notably with the pioneering Mettray Agricultural Colony in France, which helped inspire the first philanthropic body for young offenders in Britain, in the eighteenth century (Carlebach 1970). More recently Geraldine Cadbury (1938) successfully encouraged those interested in establishing remand homes for young offenders to learn from the State Observation Centre at Moll, Belgium.

Electronic monitoring: the new world order?

This chapter is concerned with the electronic monitoring of offenders ('tagging' for short) which is the newest penal innovation in the world, and one which did indeed develop in America, during the 1980s, and was then transferred to Britain. While described by both the Major and Blair governments as 'experimental', the extent to which it might still be considered 'experimental' is debatable; there is a sense in which each new generation of ever-more advanced technology will always be experimental, no matter how widespread the basic principle becomes for it is currently (1997) in use in seven countries, though it is under consideration in several more (Whitfield 1998). Britain was the fourth country to experiment with it, but because there is no particular tradition of criminological exchange with Australia's Northern Territories, or even with British Columbia, in Canada, America has, until very recently, always been the place to which we have looked to draw lessons, whether as supporters or opponents.

The *practice* of electronic monitoring, as opposed to the *idea*, was introduced in England in 1989 at a relatively progressive time for penal policy, when the Home Office Ministers, in the then Conservative government, were committed to a reduced use of imprisonment and greater supervision of offenders in the community. The general approach, more accurately characterized as 'conservative humanitarianism' than as liberal, itself owed little to direct American influences. The term 'conservative humanitarianism' is intended to express a particular standpoint in the sphere of penal policy making and does not necessarily have applicability beyond this context. The penal reform network in England (the core of which comprises the Howard League, NACRO (National Association for the Care and Rehabilitation of Offenders) and the Prison Reform Trust) is rightly understood to be a liberal–left milieu, but there has always been an influential conservative strain within it, whose commitment to low prison numbers and alternatives to custody has been as genuine as the liberals', if rather more paternalistic. In a penal context, there tend to be differences between conservative humanitarians and liberals on civil liberty questions and on the moral acceptability of tough community punishments, tagging being a case in point.

Among the liberals tagging *was* seen as an alien novelty, and early criticism of it, as we shall see, drew on deeper anxieties about the persistent 'swamping' of England by American culture and gadgetry, or what the *Observer* (17 November 1996) has called our 'cultural cringe' towards the United States.

Arguably, but quite understandably, this tendency to criticize American initiatives intensified after 1993, when a new team of Home Office Ministers repudiated what they saw as the soft policies of their predecessors and began adopting a range of punitive strategies which originated in the United States, aimed to increase the prison population and the austerity of prison regimes (Sparks 1995) and to augment the pain of community penalties.

Tagging was clearly expected to play a part in this, although it was not in itself the element which critical commentators feared most. It was the larger spectre of a violent, overcrowded American-style penal system developing here, a veritable 'gulag' for a disenfranchised underclass of young men who have become superfluous to capitalism's requirements (Christie 1992), that prompted even more impassioned warnings than usual against emulating the American 'culture of containment' (Gray 1995; see also Currie 1996; Freeman 1996; Rutherford 1996; Toynbee 1996). With the advent of a Labour government in mid-1997, the spectre has indeed waned, though it has by no means been vanquished. Paradoxically, however, the idea of tagging has been skilfully distanced from its American roots, it has won more friends, and its star is in the ascendant.

On the surface at least, electronic monitoring provides a particularly sharp example of policy transfer. Some complications do arise from the matter of its 'simultaneous *conception*' (but not operationalization) in two or more countries, and also from the uncertain role of the commercial sector in this area of criminal justice policy making. But the general outline is clear enough: in developing electronic tagging in England both new and old players in the criminal justice policy networks learned – some blindly, some selectively and some critically – from what various states and counties in America were already doing, at least to begin with.

The chapter will begin by outlining the origins and development of electronic monitoring in America, and then offer a detailed, stage by stage reading of the process by which it was introduced experimentally into England and Wales (abbreviated throughout as England, for convenience; there are no schemes, as yet, in Wales). Reference will also be made to the impact of American developments in electronic monitoring on other European countries, and to the recent impact of those countries' schemes on England, which may in the future be a more important source of influence than America. Particular attention will be paid throughout to the attitude of the English Probation Service towards electronic monitoring because, contrary to what happened in America, Sweden and the Netherlands, the Service's initial hostility was a significant impediment to its development here.

Policy origins in America

Although a case could be made for saying that the idea of electronic monitoring in its modern form originated in England it is best understood as an American innovation, for the simple reason that it was operational there for six years during the 1980s before a single scheme was tried anywhere else. The case for American origins is secured beyond argument if one accepts that the Harvard-based Schwitzgebel brothers' neglected experiments with 'telemonitoring in the late 1960s were the antecedents of the current technology' (Mitford 1977; Gable 1986). These involved a small number of offenders and psychiatric patients in the Boston area, and some volunteer students, having two-way radio transmitters attached to their belts, in order to monitor continuously their daily movements, and sometimes to send them messages from control centres. The Schwitzgebel brothers saw their work as an aid to offender rehabilitation and as a potentially cheap alternative to prison, but it was never taken up at the time, and then forgotten for two decades.

The story of how the modern form of electronic monitoring originated in America bears no resemblance to conventional patterns of innovation in criminal justice. In 1982, Judge Jack Love of Albuquerque was inspired by a Spiderman comic (in which the villain electronically monitored the hero's movements around the city, thereby avoiding detection) to promote a new way of delaying the point at which he had to send young offenders into custody. From a local electronics engineer Love learned that the idea was in fact feasible, and by the autumn of 1983 he was able to start his experiment with five offenders. It did not in fact do what the Spiderman comic had shown, or what the Schwitzgebel brothers had been attempting (i.e. monitoring movement over a wide area). Rather it enabled the monitoring of a person who had been required by the court to stay in a particular place, for a particular period, lending itself to what became known in America as 'house arrest', 'home confinement', or 'in-house incarceration' (terms which still have rather totalitarian connotations).

Beginning in Albuquerque and Florida, an internal process of policy transfer (piecemeal and unco-ordinated) ensued, so that by 1988, 32 states were involved in some form of electronic monitoring of criminal offenders, although it is worth pointing out that 46 per cent of the 2300 tagged individuals were in Michigan and Florida. Most of the schemes which have been established in these states variously monitor defendants at all points of the criminal justice process: pre-trial, under sentence, after release and during parole. They are organized from a variety of institutional bases: Departments of Correction (both field and custodial), courts, sheriff's offices, police departments and private agencies and, in rare instances, federal demonstration projects. The schemes were surveyed by the National Institute of Justice in 1987 and 1988 (the years in which electronic monitoring was first taken seriously by government in Britain). However, one of the key problems with these schemes was that a significant proportion of taggees, one third in 1987 and one quarter in 1988, were drunk drivers or other serious traffic violators, offenders who in England would not necessarily have been considered appropriate for custodial sentencing (Schmidt 1989).

The typical pattern of growth was for agencies, states or counties to send delegations to existing sites before setting up their own (usually small) scheme, although interest was constantly stimulated by equipment manufacturers, promoting ever more sophisticated devices. The impact of manufacturers and vendor organizations in encouraging policy transfer within America cannot be underestimated, as the director of one such organization (PMI) admits: 'programmes using electronic home confinement have too often been created to use the available technology, rather than designed to meet a pre-existing correctional need' (Grinter 1989: 33).[26]

Development in America was not without obstacles. There was a healthy academic scepticism about electronic monitoring in some quarters (Ball *et al.* 1988), which may have made some agencies cautious. Moreover, its spread was occasionally affected by judicial resistance and inter-organizational factionalism (Watts and Glaser 1992). However, while there was unease within some academic and judicial circles about the idea of electronic monitoring, the various American correctional services (which administer probation orders or their equivalents) never regarded it as a particularly draconian measure, and were generally quite sanguine about the possibility of combining surveillance with treatment programmes. They were prepared both to run schemes themselves and to cooperate with schemes run by others (Ball and Lilly 1996). This contrast in the occupational cultures of the British and American probation services probably reflects the deeper cultural attitudes towards technology. As described by Uglow (1996: 11), the more quizzical and suspicious attitudes towards science and scientists, coupled with a healthy (if sadly diminishing) fear of Orwellian 'Big Brothers' in British culture generally, contrasted with 'the power of scientific optimism' which pervades American culture.

Given their relatively low standing among criminal justice policy makers in this period (Thomson 1987), it is a moot point whether the American community correctional services could have resisted tagging even if they had wanted to, but in England the hostility of the National Association of Probation Officers (NAPO, representing basic grades) and the scepticism of the Association of Chief Officers of Probation (ACOP, representing managers) were to prove significant impediments to its development. Despite a history of intermittent professional exchanges, which had periodically led to transfers of policy and practice (bail information schemes from America to Britain, day centres from England to America), it would not have occurred to the English Probation Service, or the academics associated with it via research and training, to initiate the transfer of electronic monitoring to Britain. In the late 1980s the majority of probation officers were as unaware that tagging was used in the United States as they were that it had also been established in Australia's Northern Territories (from 1987); Vancouver, British Columbia (from 1987); South Australia (from 1989); and Singapore. The process of transfer to England began not with a show of interest in faraway places, but in debates and developments at home which the Probation Service had mistakenly regarded as rather marginal to its concerns.

The transfer of policy to England

Had electronic monitoring been talked about in the recognized network of interest groups, think tanks, university criminology departments and newspapers which routinely comment on the making of criminal justice policy, the Probation Service may well have paid more attention. But this network was silent on it too, and the source of the idea that tagging should be used in England, Tom Stacey, a novelist and former *Sunday Times* foreign correspondent, was a complete outsider to the policy network surrounding the Probation Service (although he was better known within the voluntary sector, which, in general terms, is an accepted site of penal innovation in Britain). Having had the idea of electronic monitoring in 1981, Stacey gathered a small group of like-minded individuals around him and founded the Offender Tag Association (OTA), a politically unaligned pressure group, in 1982 to promote it. The fact that this occurred simultaneously with Judge Love's scheme in Albuquerque complicates (a little) the question of origins and indeed the concept of policy transfer itself; I settle it by suggesting that without the prior lessons of American *practice* to draw on Stacey would have found it very difficult, perhaps impossible, to promote the idea at the Home Office (Nellis 1991, 1994).

More so than any other actor in the development of electronic monitoring in Britain, Stacey epitomizes 'conservative humanitarianism'. As a journalist, he had spent some time in a foreign jail, and had developed a deep animosity towards incarceration. This was further deepened, after 1974, by experience as a prison visitor in Her Majesty's Prison (HMP) Wandsworth. Despondent at what he saw as the failures of liberal penal reformers and leftist social workers to find a way of both protecting the public and 'correcting miscreants' outside prison, he thought up a device which would track an offender's movements, keeping him or her 'perpetually under verifiable, recorded surveillance, and with such irksome conditions attached as might encourage him to mend his ways' (Stacey 1989: 59).

Stacey had great difficulty in getting the idea taken seriously. Two separate Home Secretaries, William Whitelaw and Leon Brittan, rebuffed his approaches. Attempts to develop the relevant technology at Kent University failed to attract funding. No debate was stimulated by a letter to *The Times*. Established penal reform groups showed no interest, even after 1983 when the Offender Tag Association began publicizing the use of the curfew tag in North America. (The curfew tag fell short of their hopes for the untried tracking tag, but established a precedent nonetheless.) Stacey doggedly lobbied the Parliamentary all-party Penal Affairs Group and other interested MPs, and all the while the Council of the Offender Tag Association grew in eminence to include a former Home Secretary, an ex-Prison Governor, an ex-Director of Social Services and an ex-offender turned journalist. All of them were best understood as 'conservative humanitarians' rather than as 'liberals' and doubtless they enlarged the group's sphere of influence.

In April 1987, Stacey's persistence bore fruit. OTA's digest of information on curfew tagging in America helped persuade the House of Commons Home Affairs Committee to assess its potential for use in Britain. Concern about prison overcrowding was uppermost in the Committee's mind, and it now seemed unwise to dismiss electronic monitoring out of hand. Following the publication of the third report from the Home Affairs Committee, *State and Use of Prisons* (House of Commons 1987), Lord Caithness, a junior Home Office Minister, and John Wheeler MP (a 'conservative humanitarian' with strong links to liberal penal reform bodies) went on a fact-finding tour to the US (Wheeler 1990).

A second, quasi-academic avenue of influence opened up for the promotion of electronic monitoring in October 1987. Leicester Polytechnic's School of Law organized the first British (perhaps the first European?) conference on the subject, inspired by a member of staff (Ken Russell) who, while visiting America, had learned of developments there. This brought to Britain, for the first time, American correctional staff with experience of running electronic monitoring programmes and American academics with experience of researching them. Equally important in the transfer of electronic monitoring to England was the presence of three American companies involved in manufacturing monitoring technology: BI Incorporated, Correction Services Incorporated and Digital Products. Not only were these companies present but each of them exhibited equipment at the conference, and some even helped fund the conference. The precise impact of the conference is difficult to gauge, but its organizers (and founders) clearly thought it worthwhile, because it became an annual fixture in the School of Law for the next three years (Russell and Lilly 1989; Lilly and Himan 1993).[27]

Electronic monitoring finally got a positive response from the Home Office in early 1988, as an element in its new strategy of 'punishment in the community'. This strategy was aimed at making community penalties tougher so that sentencers would have the confidence to use prison less. Precisely why it was taken up at this point remains unclear although Lord Caithness's fact-finding tour of the United States was probably an important contributory factor. Additionally, the new Home Secretary, Douglas Hurd, may have shown a personal interest in the American scheme, and commercial lobbying may also have occurred behind the closed doors of Whitehall. Whatever the reason, the Green Paper, *Punishment, Custody and the Community*, which launched the new strategy, sought to ascertain 'the usefulness of electronic monitoring in keeping more offenders out of custody' (Home Office 1988: 12). Although it favoured the American model of the curfew tag (but not its use for less serious offenders), the continuing influence of the Offender Tag Association was apparent in a reference to the tracking tag as a 'less restrictive' (sic) possibility.

At the 1988 Conservative Party conference Hurd announced that trials of electronic monitoring would begin the following summer. New legislation (which would have entailed time-consuming and difficult debates in Parliament) was avoided because the government opted to use monitoring at the remand (pre-trial) stage of the criminal process, as a means of enforcing a bail curfew, rather than at the sentencing stage. As well as not requiring legislation, this had the added advantage of circumventing Probation Service resistance, because in England probation officers had not (at this point) routinely worked at the pre-trial stage.

The transfer of practice: phase one

The first three trials began, with some fanfare, in Nottingham, Newcastle and South London, with all contracts going to British-based firms of Marconi in Nottingham and Newcastle, and Chubb in London. The Home Office sought from the outset to reassure a largely sceptical public of the trials' worth with reminders that its officials had 'visited the USA to see electronic monitoring in operation . . . and to talk to a wide range of people about their experiences' (Clowes 1993: 67). There were, however, important differences between the British trials and mainstream American practice. First, England was testing the equipment on people of only one legal status, those on bail (i.e. at the pre-trial stage). Second, in England no 'social work' help was to be provided to the tagged individuals, which was an essential element of *some* American schemes, particularly those where probation officers willingly cooperated with them.

The trials lasted six months and were not a great success. Small numbers (50 out of an anticipated target of 150 tagged individuals across all three schemes) and significant equipment failures in the early stages, together with a high number of violations, made tagging look foolish, and very expensive compared to other community penalties. NAPO and ACOP were relieved, and experienced more than a degree of *schadenfreude* when the liberal–left press dubbed the trials a fiasco. By way of damage limitation, the Offender Tag Association claimed that the trials had not adequately tested tagging's full potential, and accused the Probation Service and the penal reform groups (disparagingly glossed as 'the Left') of poisoning the media against it. Stacey, at one of the later Leicester conferences, saw 'intellectual snobbery' towards American ideas as one of the reasons behind this.

> Those familiar with the nuances of British politics will be aware that in certain contexts the Left will use the term 'American' in a perjorative sense. Regrettably this has already happened in the context of tagging in Britain. Such opponents of electronic monitoring who belong to the Left like to categorise it as an American idea to give it a meretricious and gimmicky reputation.
>
> (Stacey 1989: 59–60)

Despite the acknowledged failure of the trials (Mair and Nee 1990), senior Home Office officials nonetheless remained hopeful that electronic monitoring would help give sentencers confidence in their 'punishment in the community' strategy, and contribute eventually to a reduction in the prison population. Commitment to curfew monitoring was publicly reaffirmed in a 1990 White Paper, *Crime, Justice and Protecting the Public* (Home Office 1990), and provision made for its use with sentenced offenders in the Criminal Justice Act 1991. Caution, however, got the better of officials when it came to implementation: continuing doubts about technical efficacy, and the continued resistance of the Probation Service, meant that when the new Act came into force in October 1992, the 'tagging section' was not implemented (Windelsham 1993: 457).

In order to understand the Probation Service's stance on tagging, it is necessary to understand their general position on the 'punishment in the community' strategy. NAPO, rather more than ACOP, disliked almost all of it, and saw the government's offer of a more prestigious 'centre-stage' role for the Service in the criminal justice system as something which would corrupt its central purpose. It insisted that the Service was concerned with social work and help, not with punishment, and argued that the intensive community penalties of the kind envisaged by the new Act would 'net-widen' (draw in less serious offenders) rather than displace custodial sentences. The rather authoritarian, quasi-Orwellian connotations of electronic monitoring were emblematic of what NAPO most feared about the new strategy, symbolizing the Home Office's lack of faith in ordinary probation supervision.

ACOP and the penal reform organizations tended to share NAPO's stance on tagging but were readier to work within the framework of the Criminal Justice Act 1991 to reduce the prison population. The framework, however, unravelled sooner than expected. Soon after implementation, sentencers, police and certain sections of the media orchestrated a backlash against the Act, portraying it, precisely because of its emphasis on keeping people out of prison, as a 'criminal's charter'. The tragic coincidence of Jamie Bulger's murder in February 1993 fuelled public anger about crime more generally and legitimated tougher talk on the part of politicians. An ideological shift to the right within the Conservative Party caught this punitive mood and the new ministerial team at the Home Office, led by Michael Howard, not only abandoned Hurd's plans to reduce prison numbers, but switched to an American-style emphasis on incapacitating offenders, keeping them off the streets, encapsulated in the slogan 'prison works'.

Within this framework tougher community penalties remained important in their own right, but not necessarily as a means of keeping the prison population down. The prospect of a centre-stage role for the Probation Service withered; indeed, its status was deliberately diminished and over the next few years its budgets were cut for the first time in its history. The fortunes of electronic monitoring, on the other hand, were revived, possibly because of personal interest on the part of Michael Howard, well known for his love of 'all things American'. 'Home confinement' was suitably punitive, consistent with the ethos of incapacitation and (although research did not favour this approach) could be used as a stand-alone penalty, without links to probation. It is therefore unsurprising that provision was made for some new schemes in Howard's flagship legislation, the Criminal Justice and Public Order Bill. Thus, drawing upon the American model, Schedule 9 (para. 41) of the subsequent Criminal Justice and Public Order Act 1994 established the basic legal framework for tagging's use in England with offenders over the age of 16. Minimum hours at a specified place were two, maximum hours 12; within that framework different places and varying times could be included in the order. It could run for a maximum of six months.[28]

A further factor in the decision to revive the idea of electronic monitoring may have been the steady growth of international interest in tagging, including interest in several other European countries. In fact, in *Invitation to Tender: Trials of Electronic Monitoring*, the Home Office acknowledged that it was 'in use in the United States, Canada and Singapore' and was aware of serious interest in Sweden and the Netherlands, both countries with ostensibly liberal penal traditions (Home Office 1994: para. 3.2). *Invitation to Tender* also acknowledges that tagging was being introduced in Sweden as a clear and unequivocal alternative to a custodial sentence (from 1994), while in the Netherlands it was being used as an alternative to custodial sentences and as a way of phasing in early prison release schemes (from 1995). In both countries the schemes were run by the probation service. This was not the model favoured by the Home Office, nor by the English Probation Service itself, and in the mid-1990s neither side paid much attention to these developments. In themselves, however, they illustrated an important point about policy transfer, namely that the process is never simple or straightforward, and is invariably shaped by cultural and political factors in the recipient country:

> One of the curious features of European development was that officials from the United Kingdom, Sweden and the Netherlands all visited the USA to assess the possibilities of electronic monitoring at much the same time. At least two of the visits were contemporaneous and certainly all three had access to the same experiences and research evidence. Yet the conclusions the visitors drew seem to have been very different indeed.
>
> (Whitfield 1997: 57–8)[29]

The transfer of practice: phase two

Three new sites, Manchester, Reading and Norfolk, were chosen for the second trials, which became operational, later than expected, in July 1995. The Norfolk contract went to a local British firm, Geographix, which had hitherto specialized in developing tracking devices for large vehicles and boats. The Reading and Manchester contracts went to Securicor Custodial Services (a subsidiary of the main Securicor organization), which had been established to undertake work in the criminal justice system. Securicor already ran prisoner escort services in London, and had run the Handsworth Immigration Detention Centre. Of interest for the process of policy transfer, Securicor was supplied with equipment for the tagging schemes from On-Guard Plus, a subsidiary of the American Digital Products Corporation.

The second trials got off to as slow a start as the first, with only 98 orders being made in the first 12 months, some of which were embarrassingly high-profile failures. The press remained sceptical about monitoring and after the first six months was urging the Home Office to abandon the scheme. A huge amount of promotional effort was put in to maintain confidence in tagging's potential. OTA invited two American programme administrators to run seminars in Manchester and Reading. It also took to challenging what it saw as attempts by the liberal–left press to discredit tagging and underplay its proven benefits (orchestrated, it believed, by the Probation Service). Home Office officials regularly visited sites to encourage sentencers to use tagging more, and although only a few magistrates were really impressed (Berg 1996), the number of offenders involved slowly began to increase. So, by March 1997, 325 curfew orders had been made.

The Home Office's strongest gesture of support was an announcement (in February 1996) of a 12-month extension to the three schemes, even before the first year was up. In the absence of demand and support from traditional allies in crime policy initiatives, judges and magistrates, it became much more adroit at wrongfooting opposition. It emphasized tagging's versatility, and played carefully into public anxieties. Following a wave of concern about the activities of violent paedophiles, for example, in *Sentencing and Supervision of Sex Offenders* the Home Office canvassed the possibility of electronically tracking such offenders upon their release from prison, and using temporary house arrest to keep them off the streets when children are travelling to and from school (Home Office 1996b). In addition, in *Alternative Penalties for Fine Defaulters and Low Level Offenders*, the government proposed tagging as a stand-alone penalty for minor offenders (an alternative to a fine) and as an alternative to prison for fine defaulters (Home Office 1996a). In the subsequent legislation fine defaulters were faced with a sliding scale of curfew days commensurate with the amount of fine outstanding, persistent offenders were to be tagged for up to six months, and 10- to 15-year-olds for up to three months. This became operational in January 1998 in two of the three original trial areas, and in new trial areas later in the year. The Scottish equivalent of the Crime (Sentences) Act, the Crime and Punishment (Scotland) Act, aimed to establish the first monitoring scheme in Scotland. These began operating in Aberdeen, Peterhead and Hamilton in August 1998.

Even though they occurred in the midst of an escalating public debate on law and order, in which the government and Labour Opposition vied with each other to sound toughest on crime, neither of these proposals were easy for penal reform groups (or the Probation Service) to resist. Levels of public hostility towards sex offenders were high and liberal outrage about the imprisonment of fine defaulters was long-standing (Prison Reform Trust 1990). Nonetheless, the government announcement that it might subject unruly children under 10 (and maybe even their parents) to monitored curfews (which produced the headline 'Curfew on 5-year-old Tearaways' in the *Express on Sunday,* 16 February 1997) met with understandable derision.

When the trials were extended for a third period in April 1997 (and the technology made available to a greater number of courts within the existing trial areas) it began to look as if tagging was becoming a permanent fixture in the penal landscape. *NAPO News* (April 1997: 3) reported on government plans to commence nationwide expansion from March 1998, over a two-year period. The fact that tagging was also mentioned positively in the Conservative election manifesto and in the more intellectual tract which accompanied it (Willetts 1997: 56) further suggested that the Home Office was now confident it was no longer vulnerable to accusations of failure or fiasco. The Conservative government, however, lost the general election just a few weeks later, precipitating (in this and a number of other spheres) some months of uncertainty as to how the New Labour government would react, because they had not formally endorsed electronic tagging, and had indeed appeared sceptical of it in earlier debates.

While in opposition New Labour had never talked up prison use in the way that the government had done, but its clear emphasis on zero-tolerance policing, mass (but not monitored) curfews for young people (ideas which also originated in America), parental responsibility and heavy penalties for anti-social neighbours did signal a tough new approach. Its overarching appeal was to a notion of community safety, which spoke to the needs of the electorate rather better than the punitive posturing of Michael Howard. Punishment was not being precluded, but Labour had not made a virtue of vengeance. Nonetheless, once in office they had to cope with Howard's legacy of a rapidly rising prison population: from 42,000 in 1993 to over 60,000 in May 1997. Circumstances demanded pragmatism and when the new Home Secretary, Jack Straw admitted in June that contracts for all private prisons (existing and on-stream) would be honoured, despite the 'fundamental objections' to them which he had claimed in Opposition, it was only a matter of time before the same logic was applied to electronic monitoring. Straw's deputy expressed it thus at a Howard League conference, insisting that:

> the effectiveness and credibility of community sentences can be achieved in a variety of ways. One of the more controversial in some quarters is electronic tagging and I certainly shared concern at the possibility that tagging might be rolled out across the country without such an approach being justified by practical experience in pilot projects. In fact the recent trials of electronic tagging have been remarkably successful, and we will therefore be extending the present pilot areas . . . I believe this has to be looked at pragmatically: does it work? . . . Let's look at [this] positively in the coming months.
>
> (Michael 1997: 17)

Although Labour took issue with the more vengeful aspects of the Conservatives' Crime (Sentences) Bill, it retained the clauses relating to electronic monitoring, as well as the commitment to the introduction of electronic monitoring in four new areas, Cambridge and Suffolk (serviced by Geografix), and Middlesex and West Yorkshire (serviced by Securicor), earmarked in July 1996 to become operational in 1998. This in itself boosted the number of curfew orders from 700 in November 1997 to 1000 by February 1998 (*Daily Telegraph*, 28 February 1998).[30] But the clearest sign yet of an authentic Labour commitment to tagging, as opposed to a mere willingness to approve and implement their predecessors' legislation, was Straw's announcement that proposals for the release, on tags, of at least 3000 non-violent prisoners, in the last three months of their sentences, would be included in the government's flagship criminal justice legislation (*Independent,* 13 November 1997). The intention was clearly to ease prison overcrowding. Proposals for a mix of stand-alone and supervision-linked measures were duly incorporated in Sections 82–3 of the Crime and Disorder Bill 1997, and even while it was being debated in Parliament (with a view to it becoming law in mid-1998), procedures for the new programmes were being tested (Whitfield 1998: 19).

Problems with transfer to Britain

Electronic tagging may only account for 0.6 per cent of sentences in America (ACOP 1997), covering 40,000 people at any one time 'out of 1.6 million on community sentences' (Fletcher 1997), but it is a significant enough presence there to be considered a 'movement' or an 'industry' within the criminal justice arena (Corbett and Marx 1992). It has been seen there as a useful tool by a range of executive and judicial agencies, who use it in a variety of ways and contexts, not always as an alternative to prison. In America it spread rapidly over the seven-year period from its initiation in 1983. In the equivalent seven-year period in England, 1989–96, the pace of development was much slower. Over and above the fact that in England control over development was in the hands of a central government department, whereas in America it was exerted more flexibly at federal level (or lower), the reasons why it did not initially 'catch on' in England would seem to be as follows.

First, there was a lack of demand and an absence of active support from elite pressure groups within the criminal justice policy networks. Traditionally, the most influential criminal justice pressure groups, the ones whose voices have counted the most with government (whether to promote or impede policy development), are the police, the judges and the magistrates, with lawyers close behind. Electronic monitoring was not 'their idea', and none of these groups gave it unequivocal support. It should be noted that at the same time they were never overtly hostile to it and, indeed, defence lawyers were quite keen on it during the first trials. During the first set of trials defence lawyers saw the value of tagging as an alternative to a remand in custody for their clients, and made more recommendations for it, 105 out of 140 cases, than any other group (Mair and Nee 1990: 45). However, during the initial period of the second trials all these bodies felt they had more pressing matters to explore with government, not least the high levels of change and accountability being demanded of them by a belligerent and unpopular Home Secretary, whose headline-seeking populism (Lewis 1997) and disregard of key professional voices alienated some of his Party's traditional allies in this field.

Second, the otherwise influential right-wing think tanks have never championed electronic monitoring in England with the same fervour with which the Adam Smith Institute championed prison privatization (Ryan and Ward 1989: 45–7). When this was first proposed (inspired, in modern times, by American experience) it was greeted with the same incredulity by the government as tagging, but within a matter of years it established itself as an important, if not large-scale, feature of Conservative penal policy.[31] The Adam Smith Institute (1989) did once speculate about the lifetime monitoring of certain serious offenders, but, as far as is known, it has never seriously entered debate on the trials themselves.

Third, electronic monitoring found no formal supporters among established liberal penal reform groups in England, despite the voice of 'conservative humanitarians' such as John Wheeler. They were, from the outset, dubious about the need for it and suspicious of the commercial organizations involved and, at least to begin with, civil liberties arguments were successfully entwined with criticism of its apparent technical failings. The increasing willingness during the 1990s of penal reform organizations to speak with one voice (31 of them organized themselves into the Penal Affairs Consortium) isolated the Offender Tag Association despite the genuineness of its commitment to reducing prison numbers, and despite the fact that some very respected individuals, such as Sir Stephen Tumin, the then Chief Inspector of Prisons (who became a member of its Council), had come to support it.

Fourth, the hostility of the progressive press in England created a climate which was, to say the least, unfavourable to the reception of electronic monitoring. While the precise influence of the press on decisions about penal innovations is hard to gauge, Dean's (1975) view that it can discourage 'subterfuge' is borne out in this case; the claims of tagging's supporters were subjected to withering scrutiny. *Pace* Stacey, there is no reason to believe that there has been a Probation-inspired conspiracy in the media to discredit tagging (see Mair and Mortimer 1996: 29), but there is no doubt that the liberal–left press in England have been unsympathetic, and have indeed used the 'Americanness' of the idea to reinforce their scepticism. Even at the time of the first scheme, a particularly acerbic piece in the *New Statesman and Society* castigated the Home Office for looking across the Atlantic rather than the Channel for penal inspiration: 'Sketching reforms on the back of an envelope in the wake of the Risley revolt, the minister has brought into early operation a clapped-out policy from the Arthur Daleys of American penology' (*New Statesman and Society*, 12 May 1989: 5).[32]

When the second scheme was first mooted the *Independent on Sunday* (15 May 1994) ran an article under the heading 'Criminals face *transatlantic* tags' (emphasis added), which informed readers that 'the Home Office wants American electronic tagging companies to monitor British criminals from computer centres on the other side of the Atlantic, confidential documents seen by the *Independent on Sunday* reveal'. It then quoted from the minute of a meeting (29 April 1994) in which the head of the Home Office Probation Division notified the Association of Chief Officers of Probation of his department's intentions:

> It is thought likely that during the trials at least, contractors will operate the electronic systems from their home base in the United States with only a small staff presence in the UK . . . The technology is now such that it is possible to operate the system around the world . . . One American firm is operating electronic monitoring from America for the Singapore government.
>
> (*Independent on Sunday*, 15 May 1994)[33]

The article wondered whether 'the British public would put up with' transatlantic monitoring. It also referred to 'critics' who 'point out that tagging is being promoted in England just when it is falling into disrepute in the United States'. Disrepute was by no means universal in America, but the same line of argument was maintained: the second scheme's unexpectedly slow start led the *Independent* (1 June 1995) to claim 'Tagging delay as *US equipment* fails' (emphasis added).

The key role of the Probation Service

The fifth and final problem facing tagging in England – the resistance of the Probation Service – warrants a section in its own right, because resistance turned eventually into acceptance, and paved the way to a new phase of development. In England, the Probation Service is both an executive arm of government and a key player in penal reform networks, taking cues from both, and its hostility to tagging was the most significant impediment to the development of electronic monitoring in Britain. A minority of probation managers, and of basic grade officers, did take a favourable view (Cannings 1989; Davies 1989), but in the first round of debate, ACOP and NAPO treated it as a direct challenge to their competence, and a waste of taxpayers' money. They hoped, and expected, that it would be abandoned. NAPO remains committed to this position (Fletcher 1997), but it was a sign of the changing fortunes of electronic monitoring in England that even in the early months of the second trial ACOP began keeping its options open. Their lead officer on tagging said:

> The Association of Chief Officers of Probation has never claimed that tagging *cannot* work. Its own report pointed out examples of good practice, where results are impressive. The problem with this is the sheer cost of success – the schemes which worked well had a high level of involvement with probation officers or social workers in voluntary organizations,

and many of those involved thought the same level of success could have been achieved without the tag.

(Whitfield 1995, emphasis in original)

A second CPO member emphasized that it was the indiscriminate use of tags at the ' "low seriousness" end of the offender market' (where greater profits were likely to be made) to which probation managers objected:

It is a pity that the electronic tag has not been targeted where it might be of value and where there is likely to be more consensus over its use; and that is with dangerous offenders released from prisons or special hospitals. Arguments about civil liberties are less convincing and the tag might then be seen as more relevant and less of a gimmick.

(Wargent 1995)

Such comments fell short of full endorsement, but they were straws in the wind. If the Home Office had abandoned tagging, the Association of Chief Officers of Probation would not have complained. But the Home Office pressed on, sometimes recklessly (promoting the tag as a 'catch-all' penalty rather than as alternative to custody), sometimes more sensibly (monitoring the movements of known sex offenders). Universal arguments against it became harder to maintain. The official research into the second trials posed a problem for the Probation Service. It noted among magistrates that familiarity with tagging eventually bred greater supportiveness and that offenders themselves found it irksome (and punitive) but preferable to prison. It cast the reluctantly cooperating Probation Service, 'at best equivocal and at worst obstructive', in a rather negative light (Mair and Mortimer 1996: 29). The scene was being set for a shift in probation attitudes, and at a colloquium (in London) on 30 January 1997 in which both English and international evidence on tagging was reviewed, ACOP formally revised its position. It conceded in respect of the second trials that 'successful completion rates have generally been good and while the range of cases has been too wide to draw conclusions (sic), levels of compliance have been higher than expected, including offenders with chaotic lifestyles, including drug abusers'. It concluded that in conjunction with 'other supervision programmes' curfew orders may well have a part to play in individual cases and, crucially, as a means of 'reducing prison pressures' (ACOP 1997).

In accepting that tagging had a part to play in 'intensive supervision programmes' and 'phased release schemes', the Association of Chief Officers of Probation did learn from 'best practice experience in the USA, where typically, 6–8 week periods of monitoring are used to "buy time" while treatment, employment or other programmes can be implemented' (ACOP 1997). But, in an effort to ensure that tagging was only used as an alternative to custody, not as a lesser penalty or as a stand-alone penalty without rehabilitative elements, it also suggested that 'current European experience may have more to tell us' (ACOP 1997). It pointed out that the schemes in Sweden and Holland (which were both understood as demonstrably effective ways of reducing prison use) were more effectively targeted than many of those in America (see Bishop 1996).

By mid-1996 more members of the Association of Chief Officers of Probation had recognized that 'tagging cannot be un-invented' and that the Probation Service would be unwise to ignore present or future developments in this field (ACOP 1996). The change of heart was partly the result of the English research results, partly the results of the Swedish and Dutch experiences, and partly an attempt to get out of the wilderness into which Michael Howard had cast the Service. It was by no means a simple capitulation to the Home Office, because it was premised on the belief that prison numbers could and should be cut. But, more than that, it was also a recognition that in a changed world ACOP had no alternative but to put forward 'a positive agenda of its own' rather than remain on the sidelines of debate and allow the agenda to be set by others.

Dick Whitfield (1997), the chief officer with lead responsibility for developing policy on tagging, was a key player in this transformation, pressing his colleagues to recognize the merits of some forms of tagging and to at least anticipate the ethical challenges likely to be posed by second, third and fourth generation monitoring technology. More surprisingly, given the lessons of Sweden and the Netherlands, he did not press for the transfer of the English tagging schemes from private sector hands into the Service. It is difficult to believe that the continued presence of commercial organizations as players in their own right, with agendas of their own, around tagging as a stand-alone penalty, for instance, will not constrain the Probation Service's influence.

The Probation Service's change of heart may have been a minor factor in the new Blair government's own conversion to electronic monitoring. In deciding to press ahead with tagging, they, at least, would not face the resistance of the Probation Service in the way that the Conservative government had initially done. But it is more likely that Labour arrived independently at the same conclusion as the Service had done, perhaps on the basis of the same American, English and European evidence, namely, that monitoring technology did have the potential to reduce prison use, and had the added advantage of making community penalties and aftercare look tougher, and more publicly acceptable. Faced with the worst crisis of prison numbers in living memory, the Home Secretary was hardly likely to reject anything that might help alleviate it. The extent to which a crisis of prison numbers, an increase of approximately 300 per month throughout 1997, culminating in a total of 63,200 in November 1997, is driving the Labour government to a pragmatic response cannot be underestimated, but it needs also to be considered that even without these desperate pressures a modernizing political party might have revised its stance on commercial involvement in criminal justice, and seen fit to accept this new technology, and to compel the Probation Service to accept these arrangements. Thus, while it was under a Conservative government that tagging was pioneered and given momentum, it seems likely that it will be under a 'modernizing' Labour government that it goes nationwide both as a sentence and as a means of early release from prison (from January 1999), creating in the process 'the largest single electronic tagging scheme in the world' (Whitfield 1998: 18).

Conclusion

In examining the development of electronic monitoring in America and England, it is clear that a process of policy transfer indisputably took place, from the former to the latter (and, indeed, to several other countries). The modern concept of tagging may have developed simultaneously in England and America in 1982, but the fact remains that when it came to developing it in this country neither its supporters nor its opponents had any alternative but to seek lessons from America, the only country in the world where the practice had already been established. Had America not provided the living proof that tagging was a feasible proposition, it is doubtful if the OTA's exhortations alone would have convinced Home Office officials that it was worth experimenting with electronic monitoring in 1989.

On the surface, at least, it is clear what the process of transfer has entailed. At a governmental level it has been voluntary rather than coerced, though it was experienced as coercive, an imposition, by magistrates and probation officers, at least to begin with. During the first trial and in the early part of the second trial the American experience was a key reference point in political, professional and media debate, although even then it was clear, partly because there was no single American model to transfer, that only 'degrees of transfer' had occurred; 'inspiration' and 'emulation' were better terms than 'copying' to describe the type of transfer that had taken place.

Although it is difficult to pinpoint when, a commitment was made during Michael Howard's tenure of the Home Office to go beyond the experimental stage and to develop tagging as an indigenous English solution to (at the time) some distinctively English penal problems: supervising released sex offenders, toughening up community responses to delinquent youth and reducing the use of prison for fine defaulters. From this point the American example declined in importance, and although it will never be wholly without influence, because of the immense amount of research data produced in America, and because it has (to date) been the site of most technological innovation in the monitoring field, it is at least possible, under the present Labour government, that dialogue between European countries which use tagging will become the milieu in which future initiatives develop.

This is how the process of transfer appears on the surface, but before concluding that we have a full understanding of the policy transfer process we should acknowledge that there may be factors involved which are less easy to see. One of these is the increasingly global influence of commercial organizations involved in crime control.

Increasing numbers of private sector organizations, large and small, are undoubtedly becoming involved in the management of crime in the United

States, Australia and both West and East European countries. Private police (security guards) now outnumber state police in most Western countries. World-wide, private prisons are as yet a small-scale development but Christie (1992: Ch. 7) has shown in relation to America, which he regards as an 'exporter' of an exclusionary model of crime control, that the provision of commercial services to the state prison system, including surveillance and security hardware; health care and food services; and above all prison construction, has already become big business. He suggests that the companies involved already have a commercial incentive in seeing the prison population, and correctional services generally, expand. Many of the companies had previously had profitable military connections, but now that the 'cold war' has ended they are seeking to tap and to generate new markets among crime control agencies.

Writing in the same vein, Lilly and Knepper (1992) had already charted the emergence of a 'commercial–corrections complex' in which governmental, professional, not-for-profit and commercial organizations were increasingly meshed together (in local, regional, national and/or international 'partnerships') to develop and deliver services. Significantly, the complex includes not just private security companies, but also subsidiaries for corporations whose primary business is telecommunications (this being where expertise in surveillance technology lies). After examining the multinational business consortia running private prisons in Britain, America and Australia, Lilly and Knepper further suggest that the 'commercial–corrections complex' is a global rather than a national phenomenon and, tentatively, that it has already become influential 'behind the scenes' in the policy making of particular governments.

There are lessons here not only for understanding the growth of private prisons, but also for understanding how electronic monitoring has spread around the world. What may look from one perspective to be a *prima facie* instance of policy transfer between two (or more) countries can look from a globalization perspective to be a case of staged expansion within one, or across several, inter-locking multinational corporations. However, it must be stressed that the extent to which future development will be driven by technological and commercial considerations, as opposed to governmental ones, remains open. Past experience suggests they will certainly be shaped by them. Monitoring equipment manufacturers already speak of 'fourth generation models' and anticipate 'spin-offs from further developments in cellular radio or global positioning by satellite (GPS) technology, as well as voice recognition systems which will obviate the need for bracelets' (Whitfield 1997). Attachments to monitor drug and alcohol intake at home were early innovations, enabling tagging to be more easily characterized as 'rehabilitative'; conversely, it would be possible to design pain-inflicting (electric shock) tags, if anyone wants them (Nellis 1993, 1994; Whitfeld 1997).

The technology for the tracking tag, which was always Stacey's ideal (1989, 1995) because it could be used with 'a far wider swathe' of offenders, including those who are homeless, has existed for some years (Renzema 1992: 43; ACOP 1996: 4) and is beginning to seem 'tailor made' for the type of control currently being envisaged, in Britain, for paedophiles, and perhaps other sexual predators. It seems likely that it will co-exist with home confinement and curfews, rather than replacing them but, in retrospect, the view expressed in *Punishment, Custody and the Community* that the tracking tag would represent a lesser degree of surveillance seems in need of revision.

We are, admittedly, moving into a speculative realm here, but Lilly and Knepper's work does raise the question of how easily events and stages in the process of policy transfer can be identified. Are all aspects of the process equally visible? Electronic monitoring does, on the face of it, seem to have involved a transfer of knowledge and technique between governments and professionals in two countries (at least). However, in view of what we already know about the 'aggressive marketing by vendors' (Baumer and Mendelsohn 1992: 54) in explaining the *local* expansion of tagging in America, it would seem unwise to rule out the possibility that commercial lobbying affected developments in England (and elsewhere) during the 1980s and early 1990s, in ways that are beyond the reach (at present) of both social analysis and investigative journalism. This does not of course invalidate policy transfer as a concept, but it does remind us that our understanding of how the actual process of policy transfer occurs can be badly skewed by too preconceived a notion of who the key actors are in the process; how global policy networks are constituted; the routes down which information and influence travels; and of the points at which, and the reasons why, decisions are made. The most visible players in the transfer process may not be the most important players.

6

Conclusion: where do we go from here?

Four key conclusions can be drawn from the analyses presented within this volume. First, there can be no doubt that policy transfer is a ubiquitous phenomenon which is having a major impact upon the structure and content of British public policy. Second, as will be explored below, a major part of policy transfer's utility is found in the model's capacity to enhance the explanatory power of other policy-making models and theories. Clearly, part of this power emerges from its dual nature as a dependent and independent variable. Treating policy transfer as a dependent variable, the contributors to this volume have illustrated why policy makers relied on foreign, particularly American, models in the development of British public policies. At the same time, by using policy transfer as an independent variable, this volume has illustrated some of the detailed processes involved in transferring ideas and programmes from America to Britain. As will be discussed below, when policy transfer is treated in these ways it is capable of bridging the gaps between macro-level, micro-level and other meso-level concepts. In doing so, policy transfer can be used to help explain better the development of many public policies, predict their outcomes and hopefully, if used by policy makers, lead to the development of better public policies, particularly in areas where outcomes are only partially understood. So, for example, this volume has demonstrated that 'foreign' models have regularly been used by British policy makers as inspirations and frameworks for the development of welfare, health, education, and law and order policies since the 1980s. Third, based upon this analysis, it is also apparent that policy transfer is occurring far more often than is acknowledged by politicians or the academic community or realized by the general public.

The fourth, and possibly the most important general conclusion to be drawn from this volume, is that policy transfer can aid our understanding of the apparent failure of public policies to meet the expectations of both policy makers and the general public. Thus, the contributors to the book variously attributed the 'failure' (or unexpected outcomes) of policies and programmes to the failure of policy makers to transfer the support structures upon which the original policy or institution relied for success; their failure to adapt transferred policies, despite their rhetoric, to the existing institutional and social settings; their misunderstanding of how a policy or programme operated in the originating system, particularly when they failed to examine its interaction with the indigenous institutional or social setting; their failure to examine how the policy or programme operated in various locations throughout the originating country or countries; and their adaptation of the policy or programme in such a way that it failed to operate as it did in the originating system.

In addition to these general conclusions, seven more specific conclusions also emerge from the case studies presented within this volume. First, rather than envisaging individual incidents of policy transfer happening in a vacuum, the theory of policy transfer allows academics to view the adoption of policies originating in other political and/or social systems as part of a growing international trend. As such, this volume has established a framework for understanding the process of policy transfer, which if applied by policy makers, can help them choose the most appropriate policy for the host setting. Third, the framework of policy transfer presented within this volume has the potential to help focus the academic debate in relation to the motives of policy makers advocating policy change. Some of the key reasons suggested in this volume for why policy makers turned to transfer were the perceived rationality of seeking readily available, tried and tested responses from other settings; the use of knowledge from other contexts to locate policy ideas, slogans and instruments consistent with ideological principles; the desire to build ideological consensus around a preferred option or idea or to test ideas that were in vogue, even if they were never 'implemented' within the originating system; and the simple desire to follow what other nations were doing.

Fourth, the decision to engage in policy transfer is seldom reducible to a single determinant. For example, in Chapter 3 O'Neill suggests that policy makers were driven toward policy transfer because of a sense of 'crisis' in the National Health Service. Thus, the transfer of the 'internal market' seemed to allow for change without restructuring the service completely and, probably more importantly, was compatible with the neo-liberal project pursued by the Thatcher and Major governments throughout the public services.

Fifth, most of the chapters within this volume demonstrate that the process of policy transfer is often far from coherent. Rather, what emerges is a picture containing many contradictions; contradictions which increase the likelihood that the processes will result in actual, or at least perceived, problems and failures. Sixth, it has also been demonstrated that as policies 'failed', problems emerged, and contradictions developed, policy makers often began searching for new solutions. Thus, it can be seen from the studies within this volume that policy transfer is best viewed as an almost continual process; where once a political system begins the process of policy transfer it never truly ends.

Finally, this volume illustrates the importance of past policies and the existing network of policies in the policy transfer process. Many of the alterations made to programmes during the later part of the 1980s and early 1990s were a response to the perceived failure of existing policies, while those occurring after the Labour victory in the 1997 general election, were within the parameters established by the Thatcher/Major paradigm. While the Blair government engages in policy transfer, particularly from the United States, the ideas and policies they borrow fit within, and are shaped by, the policy framework established in the 1980s and early 1990s.

Policy transfer and change in public policy

The complexity of policy change often makes it difficult to analyse. The meso-level theory of policy transfer helps address this problem by bridging the gap between different macro-level and micro-level theories. For example, Chapter 4 demonstrates how policy sociologists macro-level explanations of policy change have been significant in providing a perspective on the relationship between political ideologies and the policies pursued by governments (Ball 1990, 1994; Dale 1989). However, because of their abstract nature policy sociological theories cannot easily be applied to explanations of policy development. It is only when these macro-level theories of change are combined with policy transfer that an adequate explanation of education policy change and development emerged.

An example of how policy transfer can be used as a bridge between macro-level and micro-level theory can be drawn from a slight reworking of Hay (1996). Hay depicts political and social change as arising from crises within capitalism. Such crises emerge when the functions of the capitalist state (the need to protect capitalism's accumulation process and those whose interests are a part of it, and the need to legitimate the system with state intervention) are in contradiction. Policy transfer would suggest that at such critical moments, a government's range of available policies appear outdated and inadequate, forcing policy makers to turn to policy transfer to build new policy proposals. Not only can crisis emerge when events outside a political system force it to respond but, as Nellis hints in Chapter 5, the emergence of competition between different actors or institutions within a political or social system, particularly when these actors or institutions possess competing ideologies, can drive the process of policy transfer.

Finally, policy transfer can be used in conjunction with other theories to help inform the micro-processes of policy development. For example, within the literature associated with policy networks (Marsh and Rhodes 1992; Marsh and Smith 2000) the emphasis is on the role of groups, aligned by interest and resource dependencies. Similarly, in the case of advocacy coalitions the focus is upon ideological similarities between the actors and institutions operating within the network (Brooks and Gagnon 1990; Fischer and Forrester 1993; Sabatier and Jenkins-Smith 1993). Clearly, networks of both of these types are playing an increasingly important role in the development of public policies around the globe and their role in the spread of ideas, both within and across nations, is becoming increasingly important.[34] A much clearer picture of the origin of ideas and policies and how these then reach the political agenda and work their way through the policy cycle emerges when these ideas are linked to policy transfer.

Why engage in policy transfer?

A crucial element of any form of political change is the search for, and application of, 'new' knowledge and ideas. This search tends to be generated when three factors converge. The first factor is changes to structural or systemic determinants of policy, such as movements in the global economy or a transformation of state structures. These generally coincide with a second change in the dominant ideological discourse of a political system. Finally, both of these must be accompanied by a desire or need to learn about the policy and policy-making activities in another political system.

Structural or systemic changes

The contributors to this volume demonstrate that a great deal of policy transfer is undertaken in response to changes to the relatively stable parameters of policy subsystems. Such changes could be, *inter alia*, significant shifts in the economy; an election which produces a change in the balance of political power within a political system; the sudden emergence of a new technology; international trends; or shifts in the perceptions of the electorate and or policy makers. For example, Hulme suggests, the perception that Britain was falling behind in responding to the global skills revolution was a significant factor in the reform of the post-compulsory education system in the late 1980s and continues to be one of the driving forces underpinning the Labour government's education proposals. Nellis, on the other hand, stresses the impact of advances in technology in England's decision to implement an American-style tagging programme within its penal policy. Moreover, he illustrates that the belief that other comparable nations, particularly the United States, were instituting high-tech reforms was one of the key motivating factors behind the decision of policy makers to introduce tagging in England. Finally, Nellis notes the importance of a global 'commercial corrections complex' which operated across an international network, exerting considerable covert influence on government decisions and facilitating policy transfer between America, Britain and Australia.

It is in the nature of advanced liberal democracies that certain problems will be generic. During the 1980s, due to a global economic downturn, a new 'global agenda' for welfare reform emerged. Part of this agenda stressed the necessity of reducing state spending on welfare goods and services in order to bring an end to the global recession. Moreover, as part of the rhetoric associated with this agenda, a shift occurred in the language of the welfare state. Specifically, 'rights' were downgraded and the rhetoric of 'responsibilities' and 'duties' emerged. A similar process is discussed in Chapter 2. In this chapter Dolowitz observes that one of the key factors facilitating the transfer of the American CSES to Britain was that both systems were facing similar problems. Not only were both systems facing economic downturns but both countries were experiencing a dramatic increase in the number of child support awards falling into arrears. This only compounded the concerns being expressed in Britain and the US over the ever-increasing proportion of each country's welfare budget being directed toward single parents. Chapter 4 examines a comparable phenomenon in higher education policy, with both Britain and America facing the problem of participation and retention, despite sharply different manifestations in the two countries.

Networks and ideology

Most of the contributors to this volume have discussed the importance of ideology, particularly in relation to actor-based networks, in the transfer of ideas and policies between political systems. For example, Chapter 4 outlined the role competition between neo-liberal and neo-conservative coalitions played in the process of reforming the post-compulsory education system and the subsequent emergence of contradictions within this policy sector.

O'Neill discussed the impact of neo-liberal networks and coalitions on the introduction of the internal market into the NHS. The networks here included actors from think tanks; key Ministers, such as David Willetts and Norman Fowler; journalists; professionals from the British Medical Association; and US health economists. O'Neill demonstrates how this coalition of actors constructed discourses and built policy platforms which created the context for radical change, even though the US model on which it was based was an abstraction, not a tried and tested programme.

Nellis provides further insight into the role of ideologically driven networks in his study of the transfer of electronic monitoring. Here, a minority coalition with little influence in the established network built itself up into the key coalition facilitating transfer. This coalition was crucially assisted by a small, but very enthusiastic, epistemic community based around a pressure group, the OTA. In fact, without the efforts of the OTA it is debatable whether the pro-tagging network would have been able to facilitate the transfer of the tagging policy.

The process of policy transfer between the US and the UK was facilitated by a network of neo-liberal think tanks including the Institute of Economic

Affairs, the Centre for Policy Studies and the Adam Smith Institute. Every chapter discusses the role played by at least one of these institutions in the development and transfer of a policy, programme, idea or institution. The informal but close links between both liberal and conservative think tanks and their American counterparts is a key reason for their influence.

Finally, the contributors to this volume have illustrated that policy entrepreneurs are crucial actors operating both inside and outside the aforementioned networks. In Chapter 5, Nellis outlines a classic example of the role of a policy entrepreneur in Tom Stacey, who played a key role in establishing the community of experts in the Offender Tag Association. Similarly, in Chapter 3, O'Neill identifies Professor Alain Enthoven as the key actor at the centre of an active community of health economists based at Stanford University and the key person involved in the British government's decision to develop the internal market within the NHS.

Policy-oriented learning and knowledge

Finally, regardless of who supplies knowledge about policy, one of the key lessons learnt by policy makers is how to develop a policy or programme which reflects their goals. Policy transfer thus has the potential to provide policy makers with the knowledge they need to develop ideas and policies which can be manipulated to reflect their goals while minimizing their costs, particularly the cost of uncertainty associated with an untested policy or programme.

Policy transfer at the 'moment' of policy change

One of the intriguing aspects of macro-theories of the state and recent meso-level theories of public policy has been their mutual emphasis on time, particularly the length of time involved in political change and the specific timing of 'moments of policy change'. Change is often referred to as occurring in distinct cycles. This is so whether one takes a neo-Marxist perspective or a more liberal view. Gamble, for instance, refers to the work of Greenleaf in observing that there is a strand of public policy theory which views change as an ever-repeating cycle of dominance between collectivism and individualism (Gamble 1996). For Kingdom (1984, 1995), policy remains stable for a time and then is punctuated by a significant event (or 'window of opportunity'), such as a general election (see also Cohen *et al.* 1972; Peters and Hogwood 1985). Sabatier (1991), on the other hand, maintains that policy is made within subsystems which remain stable for a decade or more but are destabilized by major changes in systemic conditions, requiring new alignments of ideological coalition and new sets of policies. For Hall (1990), major policy change only occurs during a period of paradigm shift or when one paradigm is replaced by another.

However one views the 'window', it is at this moment that new packages of policy can be developed and, as this volume demonstrates, policy makers are increasingly turning to policy transfer in creating these 'new' policy packages during their windows of opportunity. When an old policy or programme becomes redundant an opportunity for policy transfer opens up allowing transferred knowledge to be put to various uses. Governments may be looking for a general model in the construction of a policy discourse, as O'Neill observes in Chapter 3, or a quick fix to economic and electoral difficulties as Dolowitz establishes in Chapter 2.

Policy transfer in the making of public policy

Policy transfer also sheds light on the policy-making process, which if used by academics has the potential to allow them to escape the straitjacket of the models which have tended to dominate the policy-making debate over the past 40 years. In particular, the policy transfer concept can help public policy theorists to overcome the confines of the rational-technocratic model which at worst perceives the policy process as involving rational actors pursuing clear goals in the course of solving clearly defined problems within an established value system (Simon 1957) and at best perceives this process as being 'bounded' by a few narrow restrictions (Simon 1997). While not as idealistic, incrementalism, which involves a process of policy makers muddling along until (or if) they reach their desired goals is just as problematic (see Lindblom 1979; Lindblom and Woodhouse 1993). Not only is incrementalism fundamentally conservative in its depiction and analysis of the policy-making process, but its account of fundamental policy shift is inadequate (for further analysis and developments see Dror 1968; Etzioni 1967).

While policy transfer does not, or can ever address, all the problems found within conventional models of policy making (Dye 1998; Hill 1997; Hogwood and Gunn 1984); it allows for the development of a more comprehensive public policy theory. For example, as can be seen throughout this volume, one of the greatest utilities of the model, which eluded earlier models, is its ability to shed light on the strategic motivations of actors in the policy process, whether these are financial, ideological or merely pragmatic.

Policy transfer in problem definition and agenda setting

Looking at the policy-making cycle more specifically, policy transfer suggests that policy advocates increasingly draw on the experiences of other political systems and/or the past in an attempt to help define problems. Thus it is common for policy makers to look for lessons at the stage of the policy-making cycle at which problems are defined. This process is helped by the growing ideological uniformity of governments in advanced industrialized nations, making the transfer of a problem definition one of the simplest and least expensive acts of transfer. For example, the seemingly global transfer of the rhetoric surrounding the American welfare state over the past twenty years clearly fits this mode of policy transfer. In fact, the rhetoric of ending 'welfare dependency', the emphasis upon 'rights and responsibilities', and even the ideas contained in the 'Clinton–Blair' orthodoxy, are now apparently universal and are all based upon a similar problem definition: the need to eliminate 'welfare dependency'.

As political parties around the globe of both the left and right converge ideologically, the transfer of problem definitions and cause and effect prescriptions will increase. The New Labour government provides countless examples of this. As discussed in Chapter 4, the transfer of the Conservatives' 'cultural restorationist' perspective on the 'problem of standards' in schools is a particularly notable example. Nellis also provides an example of the Labour government's unexpected adoption of the Conservatives' problem definition and stance on the commercialization of prisons. Similarly, many of the proposed changes to the CSA draw upon a problem definition developed by the previous Conservative governments.

This kind of transfer often, though not always, involves the remoulding of the problem to accord with the transferring party's agenda, filtering out those elements of past practice which conflict with current priorities. In this way New Labour has adopted a slightly softer language in relation to the 'problem' of single parents than existed under the Thatcher and Major governments while at the same time highlighting very similar problems, as was found in the 1990 White Paper, *Children Come First* (DSS 1990).

Policy transfer in policy formulation

Just as policy transfer can help illuminate the process of problem definition, it can also help shed light on the policy formulation process. While it is difficult to look inside the 'black box' of formulation and to identify the precise origin of a particular policy instrument, many of the chapters examine the evidence of the internationalization of policy formulation.

Policy transfer in implementation

Finally, one of the key questions to emerge from this volume is: why do transferred policies frequently fail to produce their desired effects at the implementation stage (though failure due to policy transfer can occur at any stage of the policy-making process)? In Chapter 2, Dolowitz describes the consequences of actors searching for 'a quick fix' on the 'international policy market'. It has also been demonstrated that policies often fail due to policy makers' selection of the wrong instrument or instruments. A policy instrument can be 'wrong' if it is highly politically or culturally specific like the US models of health markets which sat uncomfortably with the very distinct professional and organizational culture of the NHS. It can also be 'wrong' if it is only transferred in part, as can be seen in the transfer of the Child Support Agency. Furthermore, policy makers can also select the wrong instruments if they misunderstand or ignore how a policy or institution interacts with other policies and institutions within the originating system. As Dolowitz demonstrates in Chapter 2, one of the key reasons the CSA failed was that policy makers failed to account for the importance of the US court system.

Some of the most damaging implementation problems occur because of the mixed motives of policy makers engaging in the policy transfer process. For example, O'Neill notes that in implementing an internal market in the NHS the government 'lurched the NHS toward a competitive system but fell far short of achieving this goal'. Similarly, Hulme demonstrates that a very peculiarly British market was implemented in post-compulsory education. Policy in both these areas was driven by numerous and often contradictory motives.

Before concluding it must be stressed that 'implementation failure' is contentious, for what is regarded as a failure by one group may not be by another. Thus, in relation to policy transfer, Dolowitz suggests that one possible way of avoiding this is to measure success as the extent to which a policy achieves the goals for which policy makers developed it, regardless of whether or not these are the publicly stated goals. In this sense, both the development of the internal market within the NHS and education reform might be regarded as successes since they were intended to advance the much broader strategic agenda of transforming the structures and culture of the public sector in health and education.

Looking to the future

Policy transfer is truly a ubiquitous phenomenon which demands to be studied and understood. This volume presents a flexible and adaptable model of policy transfer helping our understanding of the policy-making process. There is little doubt that the policy transfer concept is one of the most significant developments in the theory of public policy for some years.

Notes

1 Throughout this volume the term 'foreign' is used to denote ideas, policies, programmes, etc., which are new to policy makers and emanate from another political system. This system does not necessarily have to be a foreign country. Rather, it could be another political or social unit within a country or a political or social unit operating at the international level.

2 Within this volume the terms framework and model will be used interchangeably. However, it could be argued that the two are different. Thus, all that is being claimed is that the model presented in Chapter 1 is a useful conceptual framework to help analyse both the causes for policy transfer and the results of that transfer. It is not claiming to provide a universal explanation of the cause or consequence of the transfer process.

3 Public and social policy experts are not the only individuals examining these processes; a similar body of literature is emerging within organizational sociology. These studies are particularly important for, while political science focuses upon the nation states, sociological studies emphasize the importance of the global environment. Thus, they tend to emphasize the importance of transitional and international organizations, in generating a range of legitimate policies that nation states gradually adopt, in one form or another, due to some combination of coercive, normative or mimetic forces. For more information on all these literatures refer to Thomas and Meyer (1984); DiMaggio and Powell (1991); Bennett (1992); Rose (1993); Dolowitz and Marsh (1996).

4 According to Epsing-Andersen (1990) the US and Britain are liberal welfare regimes. These regimes are dominated by a belief in the sanctity of the market and the necessity of work incentives. In these systems state-provided benefits are conditional, discretionary, and underpinned by the ideas of 'less eligibility'. Titmuss (1974) offered a similar analysis of the US and British welfare states, only referring to them as residual systems characterized by the limited role of the state in the provision and delivery of welfare services.

5 This is one of the key explanations as to why programmes based upon policy transfer 'fail' to achieve the expected results or those which were seen in the originating
   system.
6 Information conveyed to author during the 1997 ECPR joint workshops, Bern, Swit-
   zerland, 27 March to 4 April 1997.
7 For more information on the New Institutional approach see: Evans *et al.* (1985); Lange
   and Garrett (1985); Dunleavy (1991). To see this approach applied to social policy in
   particular see Skocpol (1992, 1995) and Steinmo, Thelen and Longstreth (1992).
8 The media is also an agent of transfer in and of itself. Not only does it investigate the
   policies and programmes in use in other systems but it disseminates this information to
   other agents of transfer. Furthermore the media often advocates policies and programmes,
   in operation elsewhere, that are later adopted by policy makers.
9 It must be recognized that, depending upon the source, it is probable they will claim to
   have engaged in policy transfer. It is often in their interest to do so regardless of whether
   transfer occurred or not. This is because claiming to have engaged in policy transfer
   can provide evidence of effectiveness and help justify the development of 'new' policies.
   It is also important to consider who is making the statement, and in what context, for
   while it might be politically advantageous to admit to transfer in some settings, in others
   it would not.
10 Subsequent changes have been made, most recently in the Personal Responsibility and
   Work Opportunity Reconciliation Act of 1996; however this chapter is primarily concerned with the American CSES up until the 1988 FSA reforms, as these were what the
   Thatcher government used to develop the British CSA.
11 In this context, 'families' refers to single women and men receiving child support awards
   for their children and parents living with a partner but still receiving child support from
   the absent biological parent.
12 For more information on the process prior to the passage of the 1988 Family Support
   Act see Adams *et al.* (1992); Garfinkel *et al.* (1992, 1994); Garfinkel and Uhr (1994).
13 See US Bureau of the Census (1986).
14 For more information on the shared belief in neo-liberalism or New Right principles
   between the Reagan government and Thatcher administration see King (1987).
15 Child benefit is a universally available benefit designed to help any family, regardless of
   income or assets, raise their children. Specifically, any family can claim benefit for any
   dependent child under 16 (or 19 if in full-time education). As of 1999 for a couple the
   benefit rate is £14.40 per week for the first child and £9.60 for each subsequent child.
   For a lone parent the rate is £17.10 for the first child and £9.60 for each subsequent
   child.
16 The Committee went to a conference in Australia where they learned about both the
   American child support enforcement system and the Australian Child Support Agency.
17 Information relayed to the author during a conference at the University of Manchester,
   30 June 1997.
18 These are often referred to as Title IV-D agencies for they were created under author-
   ization contained within Title IV-D of the 1935 Social Security Act. All the changes
   to be discussed in this section also fall under this or Title IV-A of the Social Security
   Act.
19 Section 2 strengthened the requirement to provide help to non-AFDC parents by making it explicitly part of the Act that help must be provided to all families regardless of
   their financial situation. Prior to this only AFDC parents were automatically entitled to
   Agency help and intervention.

20 See DSS (1990): Volume I, pp. 7–30; US Government (1988). It should be stressed that while a convincing argument could be made that these provisions could be traced to necessity rather than direct transfer, at the very least the American experience helped inspire and justify these regulations.

21 The provision to guarantee the first £15 of collected maintenance as protected income can be linked not only to the operation of the American CSES but also to the government's desire to ensure that the benefit system did not act as a disincentive to work.

22 As with the decision to protect the first £15 collected from maintenance calculation statistics, this provision was not necessarily transferred from the United States. Rather, it could be argued that it resulted from the realities and goals of the Agency. However, seeing its use in the US undoubtedly helped justify the government's decision to include this aspect of the legislation.

23 The focus of the case study is on the further and higher education system in England and Wales. The distinct manifestations of legislation in Scotland are not dealt with specifically. Yet the implications for transfer to 'Britain' or the 'UK' as a whole are sometimes drawn.

24 Information relayed to the author in an informal interview with Roger Blows, Policy Adviser for CVCP, 1 February 1997

25 Day centres provide an instance of mingling. They were introduced for adult offenders in England in the 1970s, and a modified version was taken up in parts of America in the 1980s (McDevitt and Miliano 1992). The inspiration for adult day centres in England had emerged partly from new styles of work with juvenile offenders (called 'intermediate treatment'), whose development had in turn been triggered by one London magistrate's interest in Boston's (USA) Citizenship Training Scheme in the 1960s (see Nellis 1991).

26 By 1989 there were 14 manufacturers although the market has since come to be dominated by larger companies: BI Incorporated (which had taken up Michael Goss's technology), Correction Services Incorporated (Marconi), and Digital Products.

27 Later sponsors and exhibitors consisted of BI Incorporated, Chubb Electronics, Correction Services Incorporated, Marconi Electronic Devices and Pride/Flag (a Florida-based tagging company) (Lilly and Himan 1994: 3).

28 Some American states had different minima and maxima and allowed for much longer periods of home confinement.

29 The poor results of the first British experiment with tagging was one of the factors taken into account by other European countries in their reflections on whether to introduce electronic monitoring into their justice systems, especially in Norway (Whitfield 1997: 66). Thus it is worth stressing that they actually transferred lessons from England.

30 Fletcher (1997) suggests that they will need between 15,000 and 20,000 curfew orders a year to make their operation financially viable (see also Prison Reform Trust 1997).

31 It is clear that one rationale of privatization was the government's desire to break the power of the prison officer's union (Ryan and Ward 1989) and it was undoubtedly a factor in its subsequent loss of influence (Lewis 1997). It has never been quite as clear if electronic monitoring, and private sector involvement in it, was intended to represent quite the same kind of threat to the Probation Service. But 'punishment in the community' was launched with a veiled threat that if the Service did not cooperate with the general thrust of it, an alternative organization would be created to do the job (Home Office 1988).

32 There was a serious riot at Risley Remand Centre in the spring of 1989, in which the loss of 156 prison places (Adams 1994: 163) caused political embarrassment. Arthur

Daley was a character in a then well-known TV series, a plausible but untrustworthy businessman with dubious underworld connections who, for a while, was emblematic of Thatcherism at its most tawdry.

33 This was, perhaps, scaremongering. In the event Securicor monitored offenders from a site in England, although the technology to monitor taggees across international boundaries, using satellites, does indeed exist.

34 Simultaneously, the literature associated with policy making has developed a much clearer view of the role of policy-oriented learning and knowledge (Haas 1990; Kandiah and Seldon 1996), particularly learning what other political systems are doing. Interestingly, this new work begins to conflate the old division between the role of ideas and interests in policy making and highlights the importance of 'epistemic communities' or competing groups of policy specialists, often found in think tanks.

References

ACOP (Association of Chief Officers of Probation) (1996) *Electronic Monitoring*. Draft Discussion Paper, Wakefield: ACOP.

ACOP (Association of Chief Officers of Probation) (1997) *Position Statement on Electronic Monitoring*. Wakefield: ACOP.

Adam Smith Institute (1989) Curbing Crime. London: Adam Smith Institute.

Adams, C. Jr., Landsbergen, D. and Cobler, L. (1992) 'Welfare reform and paternity establishment: a social experiment', *Journal of Policy Analysis and Management*, 11: 665–87.

Adams, R. (1994) *Prison Riots in Britain and America*. Basingstoke: Macmillan.

Ainley, P. (1994) *Degrees of Difference: Higher Education in the 1990s*. London: Lawrence and Wishart.

Anderson, C. (1978) 'The logic of public problems', in D. Ashford, *Comparing Public Policies*. Beverly Hills: Sage.

Archibald, S. (1986) 'Rescuing children: reforms in the child support payment system', *Social Science Review*, 60: 201–17.

Ball, R., Huff, R. and Lilly, J. (1988) *House Arrest and Correctional Policy: Doing Time at Home*. New York: Sage.

Ball, R. and Lilly, J. (1996) 'The social construction of electronically monitored probation in Great Britain: comparison and contrast with construction of the policy in the United States'. Paper presented at the annual meeting of the Academy of Criminal Justice Sciences, Las Vegas.

Ball, S. (1990) *Politics and Policy Making in Education*. London: Routledge.

Ball, S. (1993) 'Education markets, choice and social class: the market as a class strategy in the UK and USA', *British Journal of Sociology of Education*, 14(1): 13–18.

Ball, S. (1994) *Education Reform*. Buckingham: Open University Press.

Baumer, T. and Mendelsohn, R. (1992) 'Electronically monitored home confinement: does it work?', in J. Petersilia, A.L. Lurigio and J. Byrne (eds) *Smart Sentencing*. London: Sage.

Beardshaw, V. (1992) 'Prospects for nursing', in E. Beck, S. Lonsdale, S. Newman and D. Patterson (eds) *In the Best of Health*. London: Chapman and Hall.

Bennett, C. (1991) 'How states utilize foreign evidence', *Journal of Public Policy*, 33(4): 31–54.

Bennett, C. (1992) 'What is policy convergence and what causes it?', *British Journal of Political Science*, 21: 215–33.

Berg, A. (1996) 'Playing tag', *The Magistrate*, June: 108–9.

Bevan, A. (1952) *In Place of Fear*. London: Heinemann.

Bevan, P., Adams, M., Arthur, L. *et al.* (1997) 'Perspectives outside intervention in international transformation'. Paper presented at a conference on Public Sector Management for the Next Century, University of Manchester, 28 June–2 July.

Bishop, N. (1996) 'Intensive supervision with electronic monitoring: a Swedish alternative to imprisonment', *In Vista: Perspectives on Probation*, 2(1): 23–30.

Blackstone, T. and Plowden, W. (1988) *Inside the Think Tank: Advising the Cabinet, 1971–1983*. London: Heinmann.

Blair, T. (1997) http://www.netnexus.org/library/papers/blair.htm

Blank, R.H. (1997) *The Price of Life: The Future of American Health Care*. New York: Columbia University Press.

Bovens, M. and 'tHart, P. (1996) *Understanding Policy Fiascos*. New Jersey: Transaction.

Brooks, S. and Gagnon, A. (1990) *Social Scientists, Policy and the State*. New York: Praeger.

Brown, J. (1989) *Why Don't They Go to Work? Mothers on Benefit*. London: SSAC.

Bunce, V. (1981) *Do New Leaders Make a Difference?* New Jersey: Princeton University Press.

Cadbury, G. (1938) *Young Offenders: Yesterday and Today*. London: George Allen and Unwin.

Campbell, J. (1993) 'Institutional theory and the influence of foreign actors on reform in capitalist and post-socialist societies', in J. Hausner, B. Jessop and K. Nielsen (eds) *Institutional Frameworks for Market Economies*. Aldershot: Avebury.

Campbell, J. (1996) 'Institutional analysis and fiscal reform in postcommunist Europe', *Theory and Society*, 25: 45–84.

Campbell, J. (1997) 'A comparative analysis of fiscal reform in post-communist Europe'. Paper presented at a conference on Globalization: Critical Perspectives, University of Birmingham, 14–16 March.

Cannings, J. (1989) 'Electronic monitoring: a chief probation officer's perspective', in K. Russell and J.R. Lilly (eds) *The Electronic Monitoring of Offenders*. Leicester: Leicester Law School Monograph.

Carlebach, J. (1970) *Caring for Children in Trouble*. London: Routledge and Kegan Paul.

Chitty, C. (1989) *Towards a New Education System: The Victory of the New Right*. London: Falmer.

Christie, N. (1992) *Crime Control as Industry: Towards Gulags – Western Style?* London: Routledge.

Chubb, J. and Moe, T. (1990) *Politics, Markets and America's Schools*. Washington, DC: Brookings Institute.

Clarke, K., Glendinning, C. and Craig, G. (1994) *Losing Support*. London: Barnardo's.

Clowes, N. (1993) 'Electronic monitoring: the Home Office trials', in J.R. Lilly and J. Himan (eds) *The Electronic Monitoring of Offenders: Second Series*. Leicester: De Montfort University Monographs.

Cohen, L. (1992) *The Future*. London: Columbia Records.

Cohen, M., March, J. and Olsen, J. (1972) 'A garbage can model of organizational choice', *Administrative Science Quarterly*, 17: 1–18.

Congressional Quarterly (1985) 'Child support enforcement', *Congress and the Nation 1981– 1984*, Vol. VI. Washington, DC: Congressional Quarterly Press.

Corbett, R. and Marx, G. (1992) 'Emerging technofallacies in the electronic movement', in J. Petersilia, A.L. Lurigio and J. Byrne (eds) *Smart Sentencing*. London: Sage.

Corbett, T., Garfinkel, I. and Schaeffer, N. (1988) 'Public opinion about a child support assurance system', *Social Service Review*, 62: 632–48.

Cox, R. (1993) 'Creating welfare states in Czechoslovakia and Hungary: why policymakers borrow ideas from the West', *Environment and Planning C*, 11: 349–64.

Craig, G., Glendinning, C. and Clarke, K. (1996) 'Policy on the hoof: the British Child Support Act in practice', in M. May, E. Brunsdon and G. Craig, *Social Policy Review 8*. London: Social Policy Association.

Currie, E. (1996) *Is America Really Winning the War on Crime and Should England Follow its Example?* London: NACRO.

CVCP (Committee of Vice-Chancellors and Principals) (1995) *Funding Higher Education – Main Options for Extra Resources*, briefing note. London: CVCP.

Dale, R. (1989) *The State and Education Policy*. Milton Keynes: Open University Press.

Davies, M. (1989) *The Nature of Probation Practice Today*. London: HMSO.

Dean, M. (1975) 'The news media's influence in penal policy', in N. Walker and H. Giller (eds) *Penal Policy-making in England*. Cambridge: University of Cambridge, Institute of Criminology.

DES (Department of Education and Science) (1963) *Higher Education*, Robbins Report, CMND 2154. London: HMSO.

DES (Department of Education and Science) (1989) *Aspects of Higher Education in the United States of America*. London: HMSO.

DES (Department of Education and Science) (1991a) *Higher Education: A New Framework*. London: HMSO.

DES (Department of Education and Science) (1991b) *Aspects of Higher Education in the United States of America: Quality and its Assurance in Higher Education*. London: HMSO.

DES (Department of Education and Science) (1991c) *Education and Training for the 21st Century*. London: HMSO.

DfEE (Department for Education and Employment) (1998a) *The Learning Age*. London: HMSO.

DfEE (Department for Education and Employment) (1998b) *United Kingdom Employment Action Plan*. London: HMSO.

DiMaggio, P. and Powell, W. (1991) 'The iron cage revisited: institutional isomorphism and collective rationality in organization fields', in W. Powell and P. DiMaggio (eds) *The New Institutionalism in Organizational Analysis*. Chicago: Chicago University Press.

DoH (Department of Health) (1989) *Working for Patients*, Cm 555. London: HMSO.

DoH (Department of Health) (1996) *The National Health Service: A Service with Ambitions*, Cm 3425. London: HMSO.

DoH (Department of Health) (1997) *The New NHS: Modern, Dependable*, Cm 3807. London: HMSO.

Dolowitz, D. (1998) *Learning from America: Policy Transfer and the Development of the British Workfare State*. Sussex: Sussex Academic Press.

Dolowitz, D. and Marsh, D. (1996) 'Who learns what from whom? A review of the policy transfer literature', *Political Studies*, 44: 343–57.

Downes, D. (1997) 'Law and order futures: criminal justice matters', *ISTD*, Winter.

Dror, Y. (1968) *Public Policymaking Re-examined*. San Francisco, CA: Chandler.

DSS (Department of Social Security) (1989) *Social Security Act*. London: HMSO.

DSS (Department of Social Security) (1900) *Children Come First: The Government's Proposals on the Maintenance of Children, Vols I and II*, Cm 1264. London: HMSO.

DSS (Department of Social Security) (1993a) *Child Support Agency Business Plan*. London: HMSO.

DSS (Department of Social Security) (1993b) *Child Support Agency Framework Document*. London: HMSO.

DSS (Department of Social Security) (1998a) *Children First: A New Approach to Child Support*, Cm 3992. London: HMSO.

Dunleavy, P. (1991) *Democracy, Bureaucracy and Public Choice*. New York: Harvester Wheatsheaf.

Dye, T. (1998) *Understanding Public Policy*. New Jersey: Prentice Hall.

Edwards, C. and Wynch, J. (1993) 'American community colleges: A model for British further education?', *Educational Management and Administration*, 21(1): 19–51.

Enthoven, A. (1985) *Reflections on the Management of the National Health Service*. London: Nuffield Provincial Hospitals Trust.

Esland, G. (1991) *Education, Training and Employment*. Wokingham: Addison Wesley.

Esping-Andersen, G. (1990) *The Three Worlds of Welfare Capitalism*. London: Polity.

Esping-Andersen, G. (ed.) (1996) *Welfare States in Transition: National Adaptations in Global Economies*. London: Sage.

Etzioni, A. (1967) 'Mixed-scanning: a third approach to decision making', *Public Administration Review*, 27: 385–92.

Evans, P., Rueschemeyer, D. and Skocpol, T. (eds) (1985) *Bringing the State Back In*. Cambridge: Cambridge University Press.

Fairfield, G., Hunter, D.J., Mechanic, D. and Rosleff, F. (1997) 'Managed care origins, principles and evolution', *British Medical Journal*, 314: 1823–6.

Finegold, D., Keep, E., Miliband, D., Robertson, J., Sisson, K. and Ziman, J. (1992b) *Higher Education: Expansion and Reform*. London: IPPR.

Finegold, D., McFarland, L. and Richardson, W. (1992a) 'Something borrowed, something blue?', *Oxford Studies in Comparative Education*, 2(2): 7–25.

Fischer, F. and Forrester, J. (1993) *The Argumentative Turn in Policy Analysis and Planning*. Durham, NC: Duke University Press.

Fletcher, H. (1997) 'Electronic tagging – purpose, reliability and implications for penal policy', *NAPO News*, May, 89.

Forsythe, W. (1990) *Penal Discipline, Reformatory Projects and the English Prison Commission 1895–1939*. Exeter: University of Exeter Press.

Freeman, R. (1996) 'America's punishment industry', *Prospect*, February: 72–4.

Fundanga, C. and Mwaba, A. (1997) 'Privatization of public enterprise in Zambia'. Paper presented at a conference on Public Sector Management for the Next Century, University of Manchester, 28 June–2 July.

Gable, R. (1986) 'Application of personal telemonitoring to current problems in criminal justice', *Journal of Criminal Justice*, 14: 167–76.

Gamble, A. (1996) 'Ideas and interests in British economic policy', in M. Kandiah and A. Seldon (eds) *Ideas and Think Tanks in Contemporary Britain*. London: Frank Cass.

Garfinkel, I. and Klawiter, M. (1990) 'The effect of routine income witholding of Child support collections', *Journal of Policy Analysis and Management*, 9(2): 155–77.

Garfinkel, I., McLanahan, S. and Robins, P. (1992) *Child Support Assurance*. Washington, DC: Urban Institute Press.

Garfinkel, I., McLanahan, S. and Robins, P. (1994) *Child Support and Child Well-Being*. Washington, DC: Urban Institute Press.

Garnett, H. (1997) 'Effective and efficient governance'. Paper presented at a conference on Public Sector Management for the Next Century, University of Manchester, 28 June–2 July.

Gewirtz, S., Ball, S. and Bowe, R. (1995) *Markets, Choice and Equity in Education*. Buckingham: Open University Press.

Ginsburg, N. (1992) *Divisions of Welfare*. London: Sage.

Gordenker, L. and Weiss, T. (1996) 'Pluralizing global governance: analytical approaches and dimensions', in T. Weiss and L. Gordenker (eds) *NGOs, the UN and Global Governance*. Colorado: Lynne Rienner.

Graham, A. and Knights, E. (1994) *Putting the Treasury First*. London: Child Poverty Action Group.

Gray, J. (1995) 'Culture of containment', *Guardian*, 20 November.

Grinter, R.C. (1989) 'Electronic monitoring of serious offenders in Texas', in K. Russell and R. Lilly (eds) *The Electronic Monitoring of Offenders*. Leicester: Leicester Polytechnic Law School Monograph.

Haas, E. (1990) *When Knowledge is Power: Three Models of Change in International Organisations*. Berkeley: University of California Press.

Hacker, A. (1997) 'The medicine in our future', *The New York Review of Books*, XLIV (10).

Hague, R., Harrop, M. and Breslin, S. (1992) *Comparative Government and Politics*. Basingstoke: Macmillan.

Hall, P. (ed.) (1990) *The Political Power of Economic Ideas: Keynesianism across Nations*. Princeton, NJ: Princeton University Press.

Ham, C. (1994) *Management and Competition in the New NHS*. Oxford: Radcliffe Medical Press.

Hambleton, R. (1994) 'The contract state and the future of public management'. Paper presented at Employment Research Unit (ERU) Conference, Cardiff University, March.

Handa, M. (1959) *Hellenistic Culture: Fusion and Diffusion*. New York: Columbia University Press.

Hansard (1990) 10 February, col. 82.

Havighurst, C., Helms, R., Bladen, C. and Pauly, M. (1989) *American Health Care: What are the Lessons for Britain?* London: IEA Health Unit.

Hay, C. (1996) *Restating Social and Political Change*. Buckingham: Open University Press.

Health Policy Network (1996) *Health Care – Private Corporations or Public Service? The Americanisation of the NHS*. Oxford: NHS Consultants' Association.

Heclo, H. (1974) *Social Policy in Britain and Sweden*. New Haven: Yale University Press.

Hill, M. (1997) *The Policy Process in the Modern State*. London: Prentice Hall/Harvester Wheatsheaf.

Hogwood, B. and Gunn, L. (1984) *Policy Analysis for the Real World*. Oxford: Oxford University Press.

Hollamby, R. (1995) 'Setting priorities in healthcare – towards a European perspective', *European Hospital Management*, 2: 20–5.

Home Office (1988) *Punishment, Custody and the Community*, Cm 424. London: HMSO.

Home Office (1990) *Crime, Justice and Protecting the Public*, Cm 965. London: HMSO.

Home Office (1994) *Invitation to Tender: Trials of Electronic Monitoring*. London: Home Office Procurement Unit.

Home Office (1996a) *Alternative Penalties for Fine Defaulters and Low Level Offenders*. London: HMSO.

Home Office (1996b) *Sentencing and Supervision of Sex Offenders*, Cm 3304. London: HMSO.

House of Commons (1987) *Third Report from the Home Affairs Committee: State and Use of Prisons*, Vol. 1. London: HMSO.

Kandiah, M. and Seldon, A. (eds) (1996) *Ideas and Think Tanks in Contemporary Britain*. London: Frank Cass.

Katz, M. (1989) *The Undeserving Poor*. New York: Pantheon Books.

Kenyon, T. (1998) *The Mirage of a Choice-Based Education Service*, MANCEPT paper. Manchester: Manchester University Centre for Political Thought.

King, D. (1987) *The New Right: Politics, Markets and Citizenship*. London: Macmillan.

Kingdon, J. (1984) *Agendas, Alternatives, and Public Policies*. New York: HarperCollins Publishers.

Kingdon, J. (1995) *Agendas, Alternatives and Public Policies*, 2nd edn. New York: HarperCollins.

Klein, R. (1990) 'The State and the profession: the politics of the double bed', *British Medical Journal*, 301: 700–2.

Klein, R. (1995) *The New Politics of the NHS*. London: Longman.

Klein, R. (1997) 'Learning from others: shall the last be the first?', *Journal of Health Politics, Policy and Law*, 22: 1267–78.

Lange, P. and Garrett, G. (1985) 'The politics of growth: strategic interaction and economic performance in the advanced industrial democracies, 1974–1980', *Journal of Politics*, 47: 792–827.

Lewis, D. (1997) *Hidden Agendas: Law, Order and Politics*. London: Hamish Hamilton.

Lilly, J. and Himan, J. (1993) *The Electronic Monitoring of Offenders*. Leicester: De Montfort University Law Monographs.

Lilly, J. and Himan, J. (eds) (1994) *The Electronic Monitoring of Offenders: Second Series*. Leicester: De Montfort University Monographs.

Lilly, J. and Knepper, P. (1992) 'An international perspective on the privatisation of corrections', *Howard Journal of Criminal Justice*, 31: 174–91.

Lindblom, C. (1979) 'Still muddling, not yet through', *Public Administration Review*, 39: 517–26.

Lindblom, C. and Woodhouse, E. (1993) *The Policy Making Process*. New Jersey: Prentice Hall.

McDevitt, J. and Miliano, R. (1992) 'Day reporting centres: an innovative concept in intermediate sanctions', in J. Petersilia, A. Lurigio and J. Byrne (eds) *Smart Sentencing*. London: Sage.

McFarland, L. (1993) 'Top-up student loans, American models of student aid and British public policy', *Oxford Studies in Comparative Education*, 3(1): 259–82.

Mair, G. and Mortimer, E. (1996) *Curfew Orders and Electronic Monitoring*, Home Office research study 163. London: HMSO.

Mair, G. and Nee, C. (1990) *Electronic Monitoring: The Trials and their Results*, Home Office research study 120. London: HMSO.

Majone, G. (1991) 'Cross-national sources of regulatory policymaking in Europe and the United States', *Journal of Public Policy*, 11: 79–106.

Marmor, T. (1997) 'Global health policy reform: misleading mythology or learning opportunity', in C. Allthensetetter and J. Bjorkman (eds) *Health Policy Reform, National Variations and Globalization*. London: Macmillan.

Marmor, T., Mashaw, J. and Harvey, P. (eds) (1990) *America's Misunderstood Welfare State*. New York: Basic Books.

Marmor, T. and Plowden, W. (1991) 'Rhetoric and reality in the intellectual jet stream: the export to Britain from America of questionable ideas', *Journal of Health Politics, Policy and Law*, 16: 807–12.

Marsh, D. (ed.) (1998) *Comparing Policy Networks*. Buckingham: Open University Press.

Marsh, D. and Rhodes, R. (1992) 'New directions in the study of policy networks', *European Journal of Political Science*, 21(1): 181–205.

Marsh, D. and Rhodes, R. (eds) (1992) *Policy Networks in British Government*. Oxford: Clarendon.

Marsh, D. and Smith, M. (2000), 'Understanding policy networks: towards a dialectical approach', *Political Studies*.

Maynard, A. (1994) 'Can competition enhance efficiency in health care? Lessons from the reform of the U.K. National Health Service', *Social Science and Medicine*, 39: 1433–45.

Mead, L. (1986) *Beyond Entitlement*. New York: Free Press.

Mead, L. (1997) *From Welfare to Work: Lessons From America*. London: Institute of Economic Affairs.

Michael, A. (1997) 'A positive view of crime policies'. Paper presented at the Howard League for Penal Reform Conference, September.

Mitford, J. (1977) *The American Prison Business*. Harmondsworth: Penguin.

Moran, M. (1993) 'Reshaping the health care state'. Paper presented at the UK Political Studies Association Conference on the Politics of Health, University of Leicester, 20–2 April.

Murray, C. (1984) *Losing Ground*: New York: HarperCollins.

NCE (National Commission on Higher Education) (1993) 'Financial Support for Students in Higher Education,' *Briefing*, 17 July.

NCIHE (1997) *Higher Education and the Learning Society*, National Committee of Inquiry into Higher Education Summary Report. London: HMSO.

Nellis, M. (1991) 'The electronic monitoring of offenders in England and Wales: recent developments and future prospects', *British Journal of Criminology*, 31(2): 165–85.

Nellis, M. (1993) 'Electronic monitoring: grounds for resistance?', in R. Lilly and J. Himan (eds) *The Electronic Monitoring of Offenders*. Leicester: De Montfort University Law Monographs.

Nellis, M. (1994) 'Electronic monitoring: grounds for resistance?', in J.R. Lilly and J. Himan (eds) *The Electronic Monitoring of Offenders: Second Series*. Leicester: De Montfort University Law Monographs.

Newman, P. (1995) 'Interview with Alain Enthoven: is there convergence between Britain and the United States in the organisation of health services?', *British Medical Journal*, 310: 1652–5.

Nichols-Casebolt, A. and Garfinkel, I. (1991) 'Trends in paternity adjudications and child support awards', *Social Science Quarterly*, 71: 83–97.

OECD (Organization of Economic Co-operation and Development) (1992) *The Reform of Health Care: A Comparative Analysis of Seven OECD Countries*: Paris: OECD.

OECD (Organization of Economic Co-operation and Development) (1994) *The Reform of Health Care Systems: A Review of Seventeen OECD Countries*. Paris: OECD.

OECD (Organization of Economic Co-operation and Development) http://www.oecd.org/about/general/index.htm

Ozga, J. (1987) 'Studying education policy through the lives of policy-makers: an attempt to close the macro-micro gap', in S. Walker and L. Barton (eds) *Changing Policies, Changing Teachers*. Milton Keynes: Open University Press.

Ozga, J. (1990) 'Policy research and policy theory: a comment on Fitz and Halpin', *Journal of Education Policy*, 5(4): 359–62.

Parsons, W. (1995), *Public Policy*. Cheltenham: Edward Elgar.

Peters, G. and Hogwood, B. (1985) 'In search of an issue-attention cycle', *Journal of Politics*, 47: 238–53.

Pierson, P. (1994) *Dismantling the Welfare State? Reagan, Thatcher and the Politics of Retrenchment*. Cambridge: Cambridge University Press.

Pierson, P. (1996) 'The new politics of the welfare state', *World Politics*, 48: 143–79.

Popham, P. (1994) 'Down by law', *Esquire*: 122–6.

Pressman, J. and Wildavsky, A. (1973) *Implementation*. Los Angeles: University of California Press.

Prison Reform Trust (1990) *Tackling Fine Default*. London: Prison Reform Trust.

Prison Reform Trust (1997) *Electronic Tagging: Viable Option or Expensive Diversion?* London: Prison Reform Trust.

Radzinowicz, L. and Hood, R. (1986) *The Emergence of Penal Policy in Victorian and Edwardian England*. Oxford: Clarendon Press.

Raffe, R. and Rumberger, R. (1993) 'Education and training for 18-year-olds in the UK and the US', *Oxford Studies in Comparative Education*, 3(1): 135–59.

Renzema, M. (1992) 'Home confinement programmes: development, implementation and impact', in J. Petersilia, A. Lurigio and J. Byrne (eds) *Smart Sentencing*. London: Sage.

Robertson, D. (1991) 'Political conflict and lesson drawing', *Journal of Public Policy*, 11(1): 62–75.

Robertson, D. and Waltman, J. (1992) 'The politics of policy borrowing', *Oxford Studies in Comparative Education*, 2(2): 25–49.

Rose, R. (1991) 'What is lesson-drawing?', *Journal of Public Policy*, 11(1): 3–30.

Rose, R. (1993) *Lesson Drawing in Public Policy*. New Jersey: Chatham House.

Rovner, J. (1988) 'Child-support provisions are the "Engine" pulling controversial welfare-reform bill', *Congressional Quarterly Weekly Report*, 46.

Russell, K. and Lilly, J. (eds) (1989) *The Electronic Monitoring of Offenders*. Leicester: Leicester Polytechnic Law School Monograph.

Rutherford, A. (1996) 'Enemy behind bars', *Guardian*, 13 March.

Ryan, M. and Ward, T. (1989) *Privatisation and the Penal System: The American Experience and the Debate in Britain*. Milton Keynes: Open University Press.

Sabatier, P. (1987) 'Knowledge, Policy Oriented Learning and Policy Change. An Advocacy Coalitions Framework', *Knowledge, Diffusion, Utilization*, 8(4): 649–92.

Sabatier, P. (1988) 'An advocacy coalition framework of policy change and the role of policy oriented learning therein', *Policy Sciences*, 21: 129–68.

Sabatier, P. (1991) 'Towards better theories of the policy process', *PS Political Science and Politics*, 24 June, 147–56.

Sabatier, P. and Jenkins-Smith, H. (eds) (1993) *Policy Change and Learning: An Advocacy Coalitions Approach*. Boulder: Westview Press.

Sabin, J. (1992) 'Mind the gap': reflections of an American health maintenance organisation doctor on the new NHS', *British Medical Journal*, 305: 514–16.

Salazar, A. (1997) 'Health care reform in European countries: what are the lessons and opportunities for Latin America?'. Paper presented at conference on Public Sector Management for the Next Century, University of Manchester, 28 June–2 July.

Saltman, R. and von Otter, C. (1992) *Planned Markets and Public Competition*. Buckingham: Open University Press.

Savage, S., Atkinson, R. and Robins, L. (1994) *Public Policy in Britain*. Basingstoke: Macmillan.

Schmidt, A. (1989) 'The use of electronic monitoring by criminal justice agencies in the United States', in K. Russell and J.R. Lilly (eds) *The Electronic Monitoring of Offenders*. Leicester: Leicester Law School Monograph.

Scott, P. (1995) *The Meanings of Mass Higher Education*. Basingstoke: Falmer.

Shackleton, J. (1993) 'US community colleges and further education in Britain', *Oxford Studies in Comparative Education*, 3(1): 282–311.

Sherman, J. (1997) 'Blair to prescribe new Labour cure for European Left', *Guardian*, 6 June.

Simon, H. (1957) *Administrative Behaviour*. New York: Free Press.

Simon, H. (1997) *Administrative Behaviour*, 4th edn. New York: Free Press.

Skocpol, T. (1992) *Protecting Soldiers and Mothers: The Political Origins of Social Policy in the United States*. Cambridge, MA: Harvard University Press.

Skocpol, T. (1995) *Social Policy in the United States: Future Possibilities in Historical Perspective*. New Jersey: Princeton University Press.

Smith, R. (1997) 'The future of healthcare systems', *British Medical Journal*, 7093.

Sparks, R. (1995) 'Penal "austerity": the doctrine of less eligibility reborn?', in R. Matthews and P. Francis (eds) *Prisons 2000: An International Perspective on the Current State and Future of Imprisonment*. Basingstoke: Macmillan.

Spurgeon, P., Smith, P., Stoker, M., Deakin, N. and Thomas, N. (1997) 'The experience of contracting in health care', in G. Williams and R. Flynn (eds) *Contracting for Health: Quasi-markets and the National Health Service*. Oxford: Oxford University Press.

SSAC (Social Security Advisory Committee) (1990) *Seventh Report, Social Security Advisory Committee*. London: HMSO.

SSSC (Social Security Select Committee) (1998) *Learning from the United States of America*, HC 552 ii. London: HMSO.

Stacey, T. (1989) 'Why tagging should be used to reduce incarceration', *Social Work Today*, 20th April, 18–19.

Stacey, T. (1995) 'A tag they want to stop', *Daily Telegraph*, 22 August.

Steinmo, S., Thelen, K. and Longstreth, F. (eds) (1992) *Structuring Politics*. Cambridge: Cambridge University Press.

Stevens, R. (1984) 'The evolution of the health-care systems in the United States and the United Kingdom: similarities and differences', in N. Black (ed.) *Health and Disease: A Reader*. Buckingham: Open University Press.

Stone, D. (1996) *Capturing the Imagination: Think Tanks and the Policy Process*. London: Frank Cass.

Taylor, M. (1998) *The Modernisation of Britain's Tax and Benefit System (1–3)*. London: HMSO.

Thatcher, M. (1993) *The Downing Street Years 1979–1990*. New York: Harper Perennial.

Thomas, G. and Meyer, J. (1984) 'The expansion of the state', *Annual Review of Sociology*, 10: 461–82.

Thomson, D. (1987) 'The changing face of probation in the USA', in J. Harding (ed.) *Probation and the Community*. London: Tavistock.

Timmins, N. (1995) *The Five Giants: A Biography of the Welfare State*. London: Fontana.

Titmuss, R.M. (1974) *Social Policy: An Introduction*. London: Allen and Unwin.

Toynbee, P. (1996) 'An escape from the prison mentality', *Independent*, 24 June.

Trow, M. (1973) *Problems in the Transition from Elite to Mass Higher Education*. Washington, DC: Carnegie Commission on Higher Education.

Uglow, J. (1996) 'Possibility', in F. Spufford and J. Uglow (eds) *Cultural Babbage: Technology, Time and Invention*. London: Faber and Faber.

UK Lip Service Group Report (1995) *USA Developments in Managed Care – What Can We Learn and Apply in the UK?* Birmingham: University of Birmingham Health Services Management Centre.

US Bureau of the Census (1986) *Current Population Reports, Child Support and Alimony, 1983*, Series p-23, no. 148. Washington, DC: Government Printing Office.

US Government (1984) *Child Support Enforcement Amendments of 1984,* PL 98–378. Washington, DC: Government Printing Office.

US Government (1987a) *Welfare Reform,* Hearings before the Committee on Finance, US Senate, 100th Congress, 1st Session. Washington, DC: Government Printing Office.

US Government (1987b) *Welfare: Reform or Replacement,* Hearings before the Subcommittee on Social Security and Family Policy, US Senate, 100th Congress, 1st Session: Washington, DC: Government Printing Office.

US Government (1988) *Family Support Act.* Washington, DC: Government Printing Office.

US Government (1996) *Personal Responsibility and Work Opportunity Act of 1996.* Washington, DC: Government Printing Office.

Waltman, J. (1980) *Copying Other Nations' Policies.* Cambridge, MA: Schenkam.

Wargent, M. (1995) *Justice of the Peace,* 23 December.

Watts, R. and Glaser, D. (1992) 'Electronic monitoring of drug offenders in California', in J. Petersilia, A.L. Lurigio and J. Byrne (eds) *Smart Sentencing.* London: Sage.

Wheeler, J. (1990) 'Electronic monitoring: a humane way of keeping people out of prison', *The Magistrate,* 46(8): 144.

Whitfield, D. (1997) *Tackling the Tag: The Electronic Monitoring of Offenders.* Winchester: Waterside Press.

Whitfield, D. (1998) 'The Magic Bracelet', *Criminal Justice Matters,* 31 (Spring): 18–19.

Whitfield, R. (1995) *Daily Telegraph,* 26 August.

Willetts, D. (1997) *Why Vote Conservative?* Harmondsworth: Penguin.

Williams, G. and Flynn, R. (1997) 'Health care contracting and social science: issues in theory and practice', in G. Williams and R. Flynn (eds) *Contracting for Health: Quasi Markets and the National Health Service.* Oxford: Oxford University Press.

Windelsham, Lord (1993) *Responses to Crime, Vol. 2: Penal Policy in the Making.* Oxford: Clarendon Press.

Wolman, H. (1992) 'Understanding cross national policy transfer: the case of Britain and the US', *Governance,* 5(1): 27–45.

Index

Page numbers in *italic* print refer to tables and figures.